Millionaire's Shot

Bev Pettersen

Copyright © 2016 Bev Pettersen
ISBN: 978-1-987835-08-3
Westerhall Books

This book is licensed for your personal enjoyment only. All rights reserved, including the right to reproduce this book, or a portion thereof, in any form except for the use of brief quotations in articles or reviews. This book may not be resold or uploaded for distribution to others.

This is a work of fiction. References to real people, events, establishments, organizations, horses or locales are intended only to provide a sense of authenticity, and are used fictitiously. All other characters, and all incidents and dialogue, are drawn from the author's imagination and are not to be construed as real.

Editor: Pat Thomas
Cover Art Design: Vivi Designs

DEDICATION

In loving memory of Dorothy Anne MacKinnon
My friend, my hero, my mom

Also Available From
Bev Pettersen and Westerhall Books:

Jockeys and Jewels
Color My Horse
Fillies and Females
Thoroughbreds and Trailer Trash
Riding For Redemption
Studs and Stilettos
A Scandalous Husband
Backstretch Baby
A Pony For Christmas (Novella)
Repent (Thriller Novella)
Strange Behavior (Thriller Novella)

CHAPTER ONE

Alex Sutherland despised polo almost as much as he despised his ex-wife. It hadn't always been that way. Once, the crack of the mallet and the beat of pounding hooves had filled him with adrenaline. Now he was immune to the festive atmosphere, so weary of hiding his contempt for Rachel that his mouth seemed to have permanently tightened.

"Oh, no!" His daughter, Grace, tugged at his arm, her troubled eyes peering up at him. "Mom missed the ball again. She's going to be so mad."

He gave her a reassuring smile, subtly waving away a black-tied waiter who hovered with a tray of champagne. "No, she won't, sweetie," he said. "It's just a game."

"But she hates to lose," Grace said. "And she just switched horses and it hasn't made a bit of difference. She's barely touched the ball."

He glanced across the polo field. Rachel was chasing the rolling ball, legs and arms pumping as she spurred her bay mare. But she was also yanking on the reins, as if intimidated by the speed. The mare jammed her nose in the air, confused by the conflicting signals. However, she still tried to follow the ball, valiantly attempting to do her job. All Rachel's polo ponies were well trained—his money made sure of that—but this mare was different from Rachel's usual mounts. Faster, quicker, more spirited…and clearly accustomed to a higher caliber of rider.

"That's a nice mare," he said, hoping to switch the subject and ease Grace's concern about Rachel's truly volatile temper. He didn't remember seeing any new horse invoices cross his desk, but his apathy toward his ex-wife had hit an all-time high. "Did your mother buy a new polo pony?"

He glanced back down. Grace adored all the animals and insisted on helping in the barn, as if that somehow might put her in Rachel's good graces. Unfortunately, in nine years, that still hadn't happened. Rachel had the mothering instincts of a hamster.

"She hasn't bought the horse yet," Grace said. "She's trying her out. Santiago said the mare was brilliant so Mom wanted to ride her in the big game today."

Alex suppressed a grimace. Naturally Rachel would insist on riding any pony Santiago liked. As patron of the team, she had that power. However, Argentina supplied the best horses and polo players in the world, and while the mare might perform beautifully for Santiago, she was clearly too explosive for an amateur. The mare simply exposed a poor rider's faults, something Rachel would hate. Especially at an invitational match designed to flaunt her talented team.

A spectator behind him gasped, and he glanced back across the field. The agile mare had twisted after the ball, leaving Rachel clinging to the horse's neck. Santiago reached out and tugged Rachel back into the saddle, hiding the rescue maneuver by giving his mallet a jaunty twirl.

Alex checked the scoreboard, just wishing this fiasco would end. The Sutherland team was well ahead on goals but Rachel was having a poor game. Her three teammates were clearly trying to set her up to score—she paid generous bonuses for that—but the mare she rode was anticipating the play long before Rachel was ready. And the result was ugly.

It was never good to be over-mounted, even if one could afford the best. But Santiago couldn't control her. Rachel was always grasping, never satisfied unless she was the center of attention. Well, she'd certainly achieved that status today, judging by the snickers drifting from the sidelines. No one in the restricted clubhouse area would dare laugh, not in his presence, but the rowdy spectators in the tailgate section were much more blunt. And honest.

"That's a wild horse," the President of the Ponhook Polo Club announced, his voice deliberately loud. "Impossible for any rider when the mount is clearly unsuitable." A cluster of Club members murmured agreement and soon everyone was blaming a badly trained pony for Rachel's poor performance.

Alex's mouth tightened. It wasn't the horse's fault. But he followed a strict policy of never criticizing Rachel in front of their daughter, or anyone else. Grace deserved two parents in her life. And she needed them to be civil, no matter how difficult.

"It's a good thing this chukka is almost over," Grace said, "and Mom can switch horses. Maybe she'll get a goal before the end of the game. That would make her feel better. But I'd like to drive home with you tonight…if that's okay?"

"Of course," he said. He might have to placate Rachel

with a new polo pony but paying her off had proven the easiest way to buffer Grace. And it was a price he was happy to pay. "I'll talk to her after the match," he said. "Let her know you'll be with me. She can join us later for dinner if she wants."

"She won't," Grace said. "She'd rather us all eat at the Club. That's why I had to wear this." She smoothed a self-conscious hand over the front of her dress, a frothy thing of pink and white that seemed rather garish for a nine-year-old.

"But I really don't want to go to the reception." Her voice was low and hesitant, as if watching his reaction. "Do you?"

"Not one bit." He resisted the impulse to scoop her up and escape the fawning people clustered around them. But lately she considered his hugs embarrassing, at least in public. "We better let your mom know we won't be staying," he added.

"She won't care what I do," Grace said, and the sad truth to her words tugged at his heart. "She just wants you around."

"She'd prefer we both be there," he said. "But polo is her hobby. It doesn't have to be ours."

"Well, I like polo a lot, just like Mom," Grace said quickly. "We like a lot of the same things. But I really don't want to go to the reception."

"Then we won't go," he said.

She tugged at her lower lip, the way she always did when she was agonizing over the best way to please.

"We'll make some people very happy by giving them our tickets," he added. "It would be a nice thing to do."

Her face brightened. "Then that means we can leave

right now. And I can change out of this dress and go to the barn and check on the kittens. And I'll still be able to help with the horses when the grooms bring them home."

"Sure," he said. "I'll have the cook make us something."

"I'd rather have pizza and eat in the barn," she said. "Then we won't miss the horses when they arrive. And we can play with the kittens while we're waiting... But only if that's what you want." She gave a little shrug, as if it didn't really matter. She hated drawing attention to herself and always tried too hard to please. However, she was more excited now than she'd been during the whole afternoon at the ritzy club. And he lived for these moments.

"That's exactly what I want too," he said. "Pizza, horses and my favorite girl. My idea of the perfect Saturday night."

CHAPTER TWO

"Are you sure the doctor said the polo game was okay?" Cassie's hands tightened around the steering wheel and she shot another concerned look at her grandfather.

He leaned forward in the cab of the truck, face pale but eyes sparkling with anticipation. His expression reminded her of the vigorous man he'd been before his heart attack. And anything that took away his recent despondency must be good. Still, he wasn't supposed to get *too* excited.

"I'm not going into the Club," he said. "We'll just watch the mare from the sidelines. And I'm not talking business there, I promise."

She gave a cautious nod. Her grandfather had been a trainer and horse broker his entire life, but she'd rarely seen him this excited about a pending deal. Of course, most of the horses he sold didn't cost fifty grand. She'd been putting aside a portion of her paycheck to help with her grandfather's retirement but it wasn't nearly enough. This sale to the collegiate team would be a godsend.

Maybe his lifetime of honesty and hard work would finally be rewarded. Usually his investment in a horse's care ate up most of the profits. He was a wizard at finding horses with potential and then following up with appropriate training. Had built a reputation for being able to turn around dangerous animals, and more importantly, matching them with suitable riders. But his generous nature left him vulnerable to buyers who couldn't afford his asking price. If he thought they'd give the horse a good home, he always lowered the price and made the deal happen.

His work had let her enjoy a dream childhood. They didn't have the land or money of her wealthy neighbors but she always had a variety of horses to ride. Both she and Alex had relished her grandfather's training insights.

Alex. Her grandfather hadn't mentioned the Sutherland name yet. Nor had she. But if Gramps had been training polo ponies before his heart attack, he must have needed a place to gallop. "Do you still ride in that big field on the other side of your property?" she asked, keeping her voice casual.

"The south field? Of course. It's big and flat, and the horses need a place to run."

That big beautiful field was owned by the Sutherlands, and she was rather surprised Rachel still let her grandfather ride there. But Gramps said nothing more. He was peering over the dash, busy surveying the cramped lot of the polo club.

Clearly he'd forgotten her old relationship with Alex Sutherland. Or perhaps he'd never noticed the month that her friendship with Alex had shifted to something far different.

"Drive around to the field side," Gramps said, jabbing his thumb to the left. "By the tailgaters. There are good people over there. And we can sit on the grass and be close to the action."

She pulled her thoughts back to safer ground and

swung his truck onto the road adjacent to the playing field. Thankfully they weren't dressed for the clubhouse. Besides, it would hurt too much to set foot in there. She wouldn't be here at all except her grandfather had insisted on watching his mare's tryout game. And she wanted to spend every precious minute with him. Even though he was only sixty-eight, his heart attack last month emphasized that he wouldn't be around forever.

But her throat thickened at the sight of the sprawling polo field. She'd cherished this place almost as much as she loved her grandfather's little farm. She'd known every roll and dip of that field: how the ground was soft at the north end, the exact angle the ball would ricochet off the wooden boards...and how Alex always grinned and tapped her helmet when she made a good play.

Swallowing, she glanced across the field at the clubhouse. The Club had definitely prospered in her absence. A swanky deck and awning had been added, and white tablecloths and women wearing colorful sundresses gave an air of festivity. Everyone was smiling and holding champagne flutes, and a few people were even watching the game.

She jerked her head away, concentrating on navigating the narrow road that skirted the opposite side of the field. The playing area was the size of nine football fields — plenty of distance between her and the clubhouse. Even if *he* were here, it was unlikely she'd see him.

She squeezed the truck between a shiny pickup and a rusted sedan, breathing much easier on this side of the field. The brilliant canopy still gleamed beneath the sun but now all the clubhouse faces were an indistinguishable blur. Which meant nobody would be able to see her either.

Perfect. The tightness in her shoulders eased and she turned off the engine.

"You're going to be impressed by this mare," her grandfather said, totally focused on his horse. He pushed open the door and scrambled to the ground before she could help. "Santiago has a six-goal handicap," Gramps went on. "He's a playing pro but is also advisor to the collegiate team. He's the one who recommended they check out my horses. Everyone in Virginia listens to him."

"I'm surprised he's riding at our club," she said. "At the Ponhook Club," she corrected. This was no longer her club or her home. Nor did she want it to be. She was quite content living in California.

"He has a sweet deal," Gramps said. "Rachel Sutherland assembled a dream team." He paused, looking rather puzzled. "She must pay ungodly amounts for Santiago to put up with her."

Cassie fought a swell of satisfaction. Rachel may have snared Alex but it seemed his money hadn't made her any more likeable. As patron of a team, she could stack it with top players…and then insist on riding with them. But that meant Rachel and Alex were both here, and her throat thickened again.

"I'm hoping my mare will win Best Playing Pony," her grandfather went on, oblivious to her turmoil. "That would cinch the college deal. It's been a long time since I've been able to show off a horse in a real game. Not since you left."

Not since you left. Those words always twisted a knife in her heart, and seemed to be the dividing point for everything in their lives. She reached behind the seat, fumbling for the blanket and binoculars, craving news of

Alex—yet conversely dreading it.

Besides, this visit was all about helping Gramps prepare for retirement, and if he wanted to talk about the Sutherlands, she no longer intended to change the subject. That family had ruled supreme here for generations and had always been an integral part of the horse community. And Gramps didn't only have Ginger to sell. He had three more polo ponies back in the barn that urgently needed buyers.

His heart attack proved it was time to slow down. Training and selling horses was stressful, especially when cash was a constant struggle. She'd been home less than a week and found his pallor frightening, so different from the tanned and youthful man who'd raised her. Of course, his decline had probably been gradual. She just hadn't been around to notice.

She locked the truck and followed him to an empty space on the sidelines. She was home now, and able to help. Selling his four polo ponies would be a huge boost for his retirement. And if they needed the Sutherlands to make that sale happen, so be it.

She spread the blanket on the grass, checking the score while she waited for him to sit. The original board remained, along with the traditional way of keeping score by hand. But the familiar scoreboard was now shadowed by a massive digital display. Numbers showed not only the goals but the time remaining in the game as well as the temperature and humidity. Bold letters on the bottom proclaimed: SPONSORED BY RACHEL SUTHERLAND.

Cassie jerked her head away, determined to concentrate on her grandfather's excited commentary. And maybe even enjoy the game.

"It's the third chukka," Gramps was saying. "So we're here in plenty of time. Santiago said he'll ride Ginger last."

She nodded. Here, the polo matches were divided into six timed periods, each called a chukka. Riders generally used four to six horses, switching after each seven-minute chukka. It was a relief they didn't have to watch the entire game. It would be fun to see her grandfather's mare in action, but she didn't want to be stuck watching Alex and Rachel pass the ball back and forth. Didn't want to see their hand slaps, the team toast, their intimate hugs.

Even after nine years she felt edgy, the fluttery feeling in her stomach refusing to go away. She was no longer a local and this was Sutherland territory. The sooner she could help her grandfather sell his polo ponies and leave, the better it would be.

But this time she was determined to take Gramps with her. She couldn't bear to leave him again. Besides, it wasn't as if she were asking him to give up his life with horses. She understood and shared that passion. Her boss had already promised to find him a low-stress job, a spot where he could ride and train when his health allowed. It would all work out beautifully.

"Filming for that race series I told you about starts in a month," she said, watching a chestnut mare whose nose was jammed in the air, despite the martingale. The mare was bold and quick, but so out-of-control she cut dangerously across the path of an opposing horse. A mounted umpire blew his whistle, instantly calling the foul.

"Have you thought any more about working with me," she went on, "and helping train horses for the movie? It would be like a vacation except you'd get paid a consulting fee. Food and accommodations are free. Best of all, you never have to worry about the selling part. Don't you think that would be fun?"

Riders shouted and hooves thudded in the background, but her grandfather didn't answer. In fact, he was oddly quiet. The most noticeable sounds were the snickers of spectators beside them.

"Gramps?" She shifted on the blanket, alarmed by his silence.

He'd looked pale on the drive over, but now his face was parchment white. His mouth twisted and he struggled to breathe. Sweat dotted his forehead. Oh God, he was having another heart attack.

She fumbled for her phone, frantically trying to remember her CPR training and wondering how long it would take for an ambulance to arrive.

"I don't believe it," he mumbled, his voice so weak she could barely understand the words.

"What is it? Does your chest hurt? Just lie back, take slow breaths."

Gramps leaned forward, craning to see the field. "That's Ginger, my good mare," he said. "But that's definitely not Santiago riding her."

"Are you all right?" she asked, holding her phone so tightly she could no longer feel her fingers.

He didn't answer, but he was clearly breathing. And obviously just agitated. She loosened her death grip on the phone and followed his gaze.

Four riders wore the purple and white uniform of the Sutherland team. Three appeared like extensions of their mounts. But the fourth rider clung to her horse's neck, her mallet jabbing precariously close to the animal's eye. When the ball bounced beneath a cluster of legs, her horse twisted in pursuit, dumping her to the ground. The spectators beside Cassie guffawed.

Her grandfather, however, dropped his head in his hands and groaned. His breathing was labored but he wasn't having another heart attack. He just looked completely and utterly defeated.

"So that's Ginger," she said as understanding dawned. "But that rider's fall wasn't her fault. She's just following the ball."

"Ginger is too good to be ridden by someone like that," her grandfather said, jerking to his feet. And now his face was no longer white, but a blotchy red. "I have to talk to Santiago. Right now. We had an agreement!"

"Sure. But it's better to talk tomorrow," Cassie said. "After the game. When you've had time to think about what to say."

"But my horses don't get treated that way. And Ginger looks like a bronc. It's not fair to her." He shook his head, a tendon in his neck bulging dangerously.

Cassie couldn't pull her eyes away from that bulging tendon, imagining the flood of blood his heart was struggling to pump through his body. This was exactly the situation doctors wanted him to avoid.

"Don't worry," she said, trying to keep him calm. "We'll call Santiago tomorrow and figure out when he can ride Ginger next. How about I look up the schedule of other games? Right now on my phone. There's probably one here next week."

Gramps wasn't even listening. He twisted away and stomped toward the truck.

"There's no sense going over there now," Cassie said.

"Santiago will be busy with the game. It's best if you talk to him later."

"The third chukka is almost over," her grandfather said. "I can see him at halftime. He was supposed to be the only one riding that mare." To Gramps, a man's handshake was as good as a written contract. He honored his word and expected others to do the same. "If you don't want to drive me," he added, his voice hardening, "I'll walk. But I have to check on Ginger. She's upset. And I need to find out why Santiago switched riders."

"No problem. I'll drive you." She pulled in a resolute breath, rose and folded the blanket. His urgency was understandable. A trainer's livelihood revolved around his reputation, and her reluctance was mostly based on her desire to avoid Alex.

Right now, it was more important that she help Gramps stop fretting. He wouldn't relax until he worked out another game date with Santiago. Besides, she didn't care about Alex. After almost a decade, she was well over that pain—and totally happy with her life.

And a part of her almost believed it.

CHAPTER THREE

The sign above the door warned: CLUB MEMBERS ONLY. Their memberships had expired long ago but that didn't stop Gramps. Besides, they didn't intend to linger. They just had to cross the patio to reach the horse grounds on the other side.

"Hello, Jake," a man in a white seersucker suit called. "Hi, Cassie. Good to see you both."

The man looked vaguely familiar and Cassie acknowledged his greeting with a polite wave. But her grandfather didn't stop. He plowed through the spectators, intent on reaching the picket area on the other side. When she'd ridden here the clubhouse had been open to the public, in an attempt to attract wider interest and prove that polo wasn't reserved for the wealthy. She'd managed to participate on a tight budget but that was only possible because Gramps had been able to retrain affordable horses.

Most well-trained polo ponies cost at least forty thousand, and a competitive rider needed a minimum of four horses, along with a support system that included transportation and capable grooms. Gramps had always found her horses off the track, picking up Thoroughbreds who either weren't fast enough or simply didn't want to race. Often they'd been as cheap as five hundred dollars.

"Hello, Cassie." A woman's long fingers wrapped around her arm. "What are you doing here? Thought you'd moved to sunny California?"

Cassie nodded, remembering playing polo against the brunette, a divorcee with two sons. But the woman's name drew a blank. "I'm just home for a couple weeks," Cassie murmured. "It's good to see everyone."

"I'm married again." The woman's voice contained a note of triumph. "To Jonathon Stiles. You must remember him. He's President of the Board."

"That's great. Congratulations."

"What about you? Husband? Children?"

"No," Cassie said, her voice amazingly level. "Keeping busy with horses."

"Indeed. Well you look exactly the same as when you were a groom here." The woman's eyes swept over Cassie's jeans and now she sounded almost spiteful. "Lots of changes here. The Club made a ton of improvements after you left."

"Yes, it looks a lot bigger." Cassie peered over the woman's shoulder, keeping an eye on her grandfather as he maneuvered around the tablecloths. He didn't look sideways at the seated patrons and strode with a single-minded purpose. She didn't want him talking to Santiago without her. Gramps was often too blunt, especially when it involved his animals.

"The clubhouse isn't just bigger," the woman said. "The horses and players are much more talented…you know, compared to when you used to play."

Yes, the brunette's smile was definitely spiteful. Cassie still couldn't recall the woman's name—Jocelyn maybe—

and she didn't want to waste any more time listening to her blather. Gramps was almost out of sight.

"Luckily the days of picking up cheap Thoroughbreds from the track are gone," the woman went on. "We have a committee that steers members toward appropriate mount selection. We don't want to risk injuries, especially with the quality of our players. The Sutherland team is amazing now. Actually, anyone who rides here has to be good—" The woman gave a pointed pause. "Not like before. And we only rely on qualified horse trainers now."

Cassie had developed considerable patience working with a variety of needy movie stars, both adults and children, but this woman had just slurred her precious grandfather. Gramps was the best trainer she'd ever met, including her current boss, and she wasn't going to stand back and let anyone insult him.

"That's wonderful the players are so good here now," Cassie said. "So you don't play at the Club anymore?"

The brunette's eyes narrowed as if struggling to process the comment. Then she gave a haughty sniff. "I certainly do play. I have a plus two ranking now, only one below my husband and his brother. We won the Family Tournament the last three years in a row. Maybe some day you'll be able to watch. I'm sure my husband could get you a pass." Her gaze lowered over Cassie's jeans. "For the tailgate section of course."

"Great," Cassie said. "Those fans there are always the most knowledgeable."

The woman opened her mouth to retort but Cassie cared too little to stand and spar. She definitely wouldn't be around to watch the Jonathon Stiles team compete on Family Day. Once, that had been her dream. To have a family of her own. To ride with her grandfather, with Alex...

Turning, she scanned the crowd for Gramps. His denim checkered shirt should be easy to spot in this glamorous section. But he was out of sight. Didn't matter though. She knew his destination. The ponies were tethered to the right of the clubhouse, and Santiago and his team would be gathered there, grabbing a breather before the second half.

Of course Alex might be there as well. Unlike many players, he always oversaw each of the Sutherland ponies, not relying solely on his grooms. That sense of responsibility had been one of the things that had drawn them together.

And ultimately pushed them apart.

She steeled her shoulders, ignoring the fluttering in her chest, and stepped onto the grass on the other side of the canopy. It was halftime and the crowd was sparser here. Many spectators were out on the field, helping repair the torn turf by following the age-old tradition of stomping divots.

She forced her stride to remain confident, even though her legs felt leaden and she wished her grandfather hadn't insisted on visiting Santiago today. A groom pushed past, carrying a replacement girth and hurrying toward a row of horses. Activity was always frenzied between chukkas, like a pit stop at a car track.

She walked toward the row of tethered animals, searching for her grandfather. Praying she wouldn't see Alex. She'd vowed never to return to the Club, but sorting out what had happened with the mare was too important. Qualified buyers were scarce. Top players often owned a string of ten animals, an impossible investment for the casual rider, so selling four ponies to a collegiate team was huge for Gramps. Well worth swallowing her pride and facing the happy couple.

And their daughter.

Besides, Rachel probably wouldn't even recognize her. Just because Cassie thought about them on occasion didn't mean they wasted one moment of their privileged lives thinking about her.

I love you, Cass. But a baby changes everything. Alex's words still haunted her, the torment on his face forever seared on her soul.

She jammed her hands in her pockets. She hadn't come home to brood, only to support Gramps. Having Santiago show off the mare was critical. A top rider brought out the best in a horse while a bad rider made it appear rank and badly trained. Hopefully Santiago would agree to ride Ginger at the next match, and people would forget today's poor impression.

She could hear Gramps' voice now. Luckily it wasn't too loud, so obviously he was doing his best to be diplomatic. He was speaking to a tall dark-haired man in white pants and a turquoise shirt. An attentive groom rushed up and passed the man a bottle of water.

Her grandfather shot her a relieved smile as she approached. "This is Santiago," he said, making the introductions. "And this is my granddaughter, Cassie. She used to play polo. Now she trains riders and horses for the movies."

"If you turn out horses as well as your grandfather," Santiago said, flashing her a polite smile, "they are lucky to have you." He took a swig of water and looked back at her grandfather. "I intended to ride your mare today but we had to shuffle some horses at the last minute."

"But you'll give Ginger a try in next week's game?" Gramps asked.

"Yes," Santiago said. "Rachel no longer wants to ride her so that won't be a problem."

"Good," Gramps said, blowing out a sigh of relief. "Because we both know the mare is much better than what people saw today. It's unfortunate *she* fell off."

Santiago gave a diplomatic smile. His eyes cut beyond her grandfather and his teeth flashed even whiter. It was the type of dazzling smile that movie stars perfected. Cassie had developed a knack for assessing genuine emotion and she sensed right away this man was a master at turning on the charm. He was focused on impressing someone…but obviously not them.

She followed his gaze, looking past the muscled hindquarters of the line of polo ponies, past the smell of boot polish and horse sweat and saddle soap. The excited chatter faded away. And she could only stare.

Rachel Sutherland must have changed her clothes because despite her tumble to the grass, her white pants were immaculate. So was her face. Her figure. Her hair. She hadn't turned fat or ugly. In fact, she looked exactly the same. If Ralph Lauren needed a glamorous female polo model, she definitely ticked all the boxes. No wonder Alex had chosen her.

Cassie jerked her head away. She didn't see Alex. Nor did she want to. She just wanted to escape these beautiful people and go home with her grandfather and figure out the best way to help him retire. A way that would ensure they'd never have to live apart again.

Next week Santiago would ride their mare and Ginger

would have a brilliant game and then the college would buy Gramps' horses and he could finally shed his responsibility. He'd never been away from his barn for more than a weekend. Had never even had a real vacation.

He'd enjoy hanging out with her on the movie set. He'd still be involved with horses but he wouldn't have to worry about his next customer. Wouldn't have to get up every morning wondering if a horse would sell in time to pay the feed bill. That freedom alone would ease his stress.

Her boss was always looking for experienced horsemen. They could compare training methods and talk about animals they'd trained and she'd no longer ache to be closer to Gramps. They'd be able to make a real home again and they'd both grow to love California. She opened her hands, determinedly pressing her sweaty palms against her jeans.

"Mr. Edwards? Jake Edwards?"

The voice behind them was imperious, with a slight New York accent, almost exactly as Cassie remembered. She swallowed and turned, wondering if Rachel would even recognize her.

But the stunning woman standing in front of them stared only at Gramps. "I want to advise you that our committee will be sending out official notice," Rachel said. "Your mare is dangerous. Totally unsuitable for this game. She shouldn't be allowed to step foot on any polo field."

"I'll give his mare another chance next week," Santiago said quickly. "She might have been a little off today."

"Absolutely not," Rachel said, her cold eyes still locked on Gramps. "She almost killed me. You must take her back. Our club can't waste time on inferior animals…or trainers."

Cassie jerked forward at the slur, but her grandfather grabbed her arm.

"Let's go, Santiago," Rachel went on, not deigning to look at Cassie. "We have to mount now."

She strode away, swinging her mallet like a weapon.

Cassie's cheeks felt hot and it hurt to breathe. Her grandfather's hand was digging into her arm and Santiago just stared, clearly surprised but unwilling to annoy his patron.

"I'm sorry," Santiago said slowly. "But it seems best if you take the mare home. We can try out your horses next year."

"But the college is buying now," her grandfather said.

"There is nothing I can do." Santiago gave them both a dismissive nod, but his expression remained shuttered, his polite smile not reaching his eyes. He turned and followed Rachel like a pet dog.

"Don't let those people bother you," Cassie said, her voice quivering. "You're a great trainer. He knows that. Rachel knows it too. We'll find another rider. Then everyone will see how good Ginger really is."

"No," Gramps said. He still held her forearm. But his grip had weakened and he seemed to be clutching her for balance rather than to restrain. "We need to take Ginger home. Rachel has too much clout. No player would dare give my horses a chance now. And I don't blame them."

"But that's not fair—" Cassie pulled in a painful gulp and stopped talking. Life wasn't fair. She knew that as well as Gramps. And she was supposed to be the strong one now. "Of course," she said, pasting on a reassuring smile. "We'll take Ginger home and figure out another way. We'll find a different polo club."

She glanced over her shoulder. Rachel was adjusting a knee guard while a groom knelt at her feet, giving her immaculate leather boots one last polish. She looked objective and totally focused on polo. She probably hadn't intended to insult Gramps like that. Didn't realize how disastrous it was to have a horse black listed.

Maybe the situation wasn't so bad. Santiago could talk to her. Explain that it would be a good move for him to ride Ginger. Everyone wanted the best horses for their team, and clearly the woman didn't even remember Cassie.

But as she considered that possibility, Rachel's head swiveled. Her eyes locked with Cassie's and her expression turned mocking. Despite the woman's physical perfection there was nothing beautiful about her now. In fact, she looked downright malicious.

Cassie stared back, refusing to be the first to look away. But despite the warmth of the sun, her skin felt cold, clammy. Because it was obvious Rachel did remember her. And it was also clear that despite Cassie's good intentions, her presence hadn't helped Gramps. Not one bit. In fact, it was apparent that coming home had only helped draw the ire of a very powerful and vindictive woman.

CHAPTER FOUR

The clubhouse swelled with applause as Rachel and Santiago cantered their fancy polo ponies back onto the field. A mounted umpire prepared to throw the ball out and start the second half.

"Let's go home," Cassie repeated.

She wasn't interested in watching the rest of the game and couldn't understand why Gramps still lingered by the terrace. Already club members gave them a wide berth, as if aware of the Sutherland black list and loath to fraternize with the enemy.

"No," Gramps said, his stubborn gaze locked on the row of tethered horses. "I need to check Ginger before we leave. I couldn't get close to her before. But she looked lathered so I want to make sure they're cooling her out okay. After the throw-out, I can slip back and see her."

"Okay. But we better not stay long." She still had to drive her grandfather home, hook up his old trailer then hurry back and pick up Ginger before everyone left. She had the horrible suspicion Rachel was capable of deserting the mare at the polo field. And Ginger would hate being left alone. Any horse would.

She scanned the riders on the field. At least she hadn't bumped into Alex. Odd he wasn't playing today. A relief really. Still, she couldn't control a flash of anger. While her grandfather had never moved in the same social circles as the Sutherlands, he knew them well.

Gramps had always welcomed Alex at his barn, and in his home. At one time he'd been Alex's mentor, more like an uncle than a trainer. Yet when Gramps needed Alex's support most, the man turned invisible.

"Where's Alex?" she asked, struggling to keep her voice light. "Does he play on a different team?"

"I don't know." Gramps shrugged, his gaze still locked on the picketed ponies. "Haven't seen him in years. I imagine he's in the clubhouse."

Cassie's mouth lifted in a rueful smile. Her grandfather rarely worried about people. And he no longer seemed upset about how Rachel had trashed his mare and the repercussions that would create. He was only thinking about Ginger's welfare and whether Rachel's grooms were cooling her out properly.

He always worried about the horses first, emphasizing that if a rider was hot and thirsty, the horse probably was too. Alex hadn't been spared the lectures. But unlike some people, he'd seemed to relish them, nodding and absorbing every word. Probably because his own parents had left him alone with a string of disinterested housekeepers, and he'd appreciated any sort of attention.

She jammed her hands in her back pockets, watching as the umpire threw the ball in to start the second half. Santiago quickly gained possession and lobbed Rachel a perfect pass. Rachel swung her mallet and the ball trickled between the goalposts. The clubhouse crowd cheered as if it had been a world-caliber shot.

"Look how she scores when riding a well-trained

horse," someone said.

"Yes," a man in a dark blazer replied. "Her last mount stunk. The kind of horse that's good for nothing but dog food."

Gramps flinched and the horror on his kind face tugged at Cassie's heart. "Let's check Ginger now," she said, sending the idiot in the blazer a withering glare.

They slipped past the PLAYERS AND GROOMS ONLY sign and behind the row of horses. The visiting team had brought extra animals so there were over twenty polo ponies tethered in a line beneath a shaded roof. A few were blanketed with cotton coolers designed to keep their muscles from stiffening. Grooms scurried everywhere, lugging brushes, buckets and bandages. Most of the animals tugged contentedly at their hay nets, aware their time on the polo field was over and that soon they'd be loaded on the trailers and returned to their respective stables.

Then the color of the bandages and blankets changed to an imposing purple and gold. The Sutherland team colors. The horses in this section had a much more elaborate setup with open-air stalls and matching purple hay nets stuffed with alfalfa. Their long tails had been released from their polo knots and brushed out to a silky shine, and it was obvious they received the best of care.

But Gramps' brow furrowed. "I don't see Ginger," he said. "I recognize these three horses from that last chukka. She should be tied with them. But where is she?"

His words trailed off in a disbelieving hiss as both he and Cassie spotted his horse at the same time.

Ginger was tied to the back of a portable toilet a hundred yards from the other animals. She had no shade or hay or water, and a short rope forced her head unnaturally high. Her braided tail was still tied up in a game knot allowing the flies to feast undisturbed.

"Dammit." Her grandfather charged forward. At the sound of his voice, Ginger nickered, a heartrending sound of welcome and relief.

"I'm sorry, girl." He fumbled to untie her rope. But his fingers were shaking so much he couldn't manage the knot.

"Let me do that, Gramps." Cassie gently pushed his hands away and released the knot. She couldn't bear to look at her grandfather's face. Didn't want to see his torment. If Rachel had wanted to hurt him, this had been effective, even more than slandering his training abilities. But tying a hot horse out in the sun after the mare had valiantly galloped around a field trying to please her inept rider was not only cruel, it was criminal.

It was a good thing Gramps had insisted on checking. At least they'd arrived in time. It had only been fifteen minutes since Ginger walked off the field. They could lead her around, give her slow sips of water and brush out her tail so she could swish away the hordes of flies.

Cassie's eyes narrowed on the mare's ribs. There were so many clustering flies they resembled a moving cloud of black. She waved her hand and they rose in a mass—revealing blood-red gashes.

She gasped then forced her words out between gritted teeth. "I'm going to cool out Ginger. And then I'm staying to talk to Rachel. This is despicable. Hey!" she called, gesturing at a passing groom. "What the hell are you guys doing? Did you forget about this mare?"

The groom shuffled over, not meeting her eyes. "Rachel

wanted that mare to be left alone," he said. "And she tied her like that. Wanted to teach her a lesson."

"Fortunately she's not her horse to teach," Cassie said, pulling out the camera on her phone. "We need a bucket of water and some hay and ointment. And I want someone on the committee to come over right away and witness this abuse."

"But her sides were bloody when she came," the groom said, his voice earnest now. "Some backwoods trainer named Jake Edwards had the mare, and Rachel was just trying to rescue the horse. Even the vet saw the marks. It's all been documented. No one will ever let that guy's animals on a polo field again. And Rachel is going to post it on the website so everyone knows."

Cassie's fingers turned so numb she almost dropped her phone. This was being blamed on Gramps. She'd always known Rachel was crafty, but this was brilliantly evil.

"Just bring me the water and ointment, please," she said, trying to gather her composure before daring to look at Gramps. She could already feel his confusion, sense him shriveling beside her. She could even imagine his heart pounding in horror. And *that* couldn't be healthy.

Unfortunately there was little she could do to make him feel better—except wait for the end of the game and hope for a chance to confront Rachel.

CHAPTER FIVE

"Rachel just wants to win," Santiago said, cradling his helmet and swiping the sweat from his forehead. "Good players are competitive like that. She had a tough game in the first half and took it out on the mare. That's normal."

"It's not normal," Cassie snapped. The end of a grueling polo match wasn't the best time to confront Santiago but Rachel had tossed her reins to a groom and disappeared into the clubhouse and Cassie was too incensed to leave without saying something.

"She overrode Ginger," Cassie went on. "Cut up her sides with spurs, then left her standing in the sun. Tied to a stinky portable. It was cruel." She pulled in a shaky breath, hating the telltale quiver in her voice. "She told the grooms to leave her. Then blamed her condition on my grandfather. And Ginger was your responsibility. You're the one who was working with her all month. You were the one supposed to ride her today."

"And I'd planned to," Santiago said smoothly. "But Rachel insisted on switching. And we wouldn't have left the mare tied here any longer. In fact, she'll be trailered safely back to the Sutherland Estate along with the rest of the horses. Her legs will be wrapped and she can have a nice bran mash…and you can pick her up there and take her home."

"That's just great." Cassie's throat closed so tightly it hurt to talk. "So Ginger doesn't get a second chance? And now no club will ever look at Gramps' horses. He devoted his life to training, to horses—"

"It's unfortunate it worked out like this." Santiago tugged off his gloves, flexing his lean fingers. "Sorry but there's nothing I can do."

He didn't sound at all sorry and Cassie glared at him until he looked away.

"Why don't we talk next year," he added. "People have short memories. And the college might need another horse then. It's not such a big deal."

"But my grandfather has four polo ponies that he needs to sell now. And you riding Ginger was the agreement. So it is a big deal."

"Look, I apologize. But Rachel doesn't like that mare. So there's nothing more to discuss." He slapped his gloves against his palm, the crack loud in the still air. "Now I must shower and attend a reception. I'll do what I can. But your grandfather and I had nothing in writing."

He inclined his head and walked away, pausing to give last-minute instructions to a slim groom loading saddles onto a trailer. Santiago's teeth gleamed in a confident smile, and the female groom looked up at him like he was a god. He was undoubtedly good looking with a real talent for polo—something Cassie could usually appreciate—but at this moment he looked more wolfish than handsome, the perfect henchman for someone like Rachel.

Cassie pulled in a ragged breath, forcing herself to relax before walking away and following the line of horses. It wouldn't help Gramps to see her upset. And right now he'd be focused on Ginger, not Santiago's scruples. Or lack of them.

She found her grandfather bent over Ginger's legs, gently checking the horse's tendons. "There's no heat," he said, glancing up and giving Cassie a relieved nod. "She seems fine, other than the abrasions."

And the possible damage to her mind. It wasn't always physical. Some horses struggled mentally after a bad experience. But Cassie didn't voice her fears. There was no telling how Rachel's riding might have impacted the mare. Some animals could shake off a bad experience easier than others. And they had been relatively lucky. Not only did Rachel have rough hands, she was also reckless with her mallet. So it was a relief Ginger's legs seemed unharmed.

"Santiago said they'd take her back to Sutherlands with the rest of the ponies," Cassie said brightly, hoping her lip didn't curl at the mention of the man's name. "He won't have another chance to ride Ginger this summer though. So I'll hook up your trailer and pick her up tonight." *So she's safely off the Sutherland Estate before Rachel arrives home.*

"Okay," Gramps said. "But let's stay with her. Until she's loaded and away from here."

Cassie nodded. Obviously her grandfather didn't trust Rachel either and he had excellent instincts. But it was unsettling to fear for the safety of an animal and it wasn't only Rachel they had to worry about. Santiago was on the Sutherland payroll too, along with countless others. And in this area the Sutherland family ruled supreme.

She peered over her shoulder. On the surface everything appeared normal. Music and laughter filtered beyond the elaborate glass walls of the clubhouse. The sun hadn't set but already the patio glowed with welcoming white lights. However the skin on her neck prickled as though everyone behind the glass was watching, and conspiring.

"Rachel and Santiago won't get near Ginger again," Cassie said, trying to reassure herself as well as Gramps. "I'll pick her up long before they leave the reception." She paused, struggling to talk around the guilt balling in her throat. "I'm so sorry. I'm afraid this is my fault. Rachel—"

"Doesn't like you much," her grandfather said. "I know."

"I should have stayed away," Cassie said. "If I hadn't come home this never would have happened. And Santiago would have ridden Ginger today and she would have been a star, instead of topping Rachel's shit list."

"But I'm glad you came back." Gramps fiddled with his belt, taking a moment to hike up his pants, as if embarrassed but determined to speak. "You never spoke much about Alex or Rachel. Never once asked about them. Was she the reason you left?"

"I found a job at the equine center in West Virginia," Cassie said. "You know that."

"But you and Alex were such good friends. He might have made you chase his polo balls and was always teasing, but he looked out for you. And that last summer I thought maybe you were more than friends?"

Cassie averted her head, unnecessarily tugging the water bucket a half inch closer to Ginger's front feet. "That was a long time ago," she said. "I barely remember."

She didn't remember the night she and Alex had sat up with a colicy horse and ended up in each other's arms. Couldn't remember his passionate kiss or the tenderness of his touch or how he'd spread his expensive jacket on the hay so it wouldn't prick her skin. How he whispered that she was the best thing in his life. And that he loved her.

"He came by a few times," Gramps said. "After you left. Tried to give me money. I suspected he felt guilty about something."

She squeezed her eyes shut. Alex had tried to give her money too. But it hadn't been his money she wanted.

"I sent him packing," her grandfather added. "Said I didn't want to see him around ever again. Didn't really mean it. I was just upset you'd moved away. He was a good kid, and a big help. But he never rode in that south field again."

Cassie's head jerked up. "But that's the field the Sutherlands groomed for polo. We always rode there… He always rode there."

"And I still do," Gramps said, his eyes twinkling now. "Apparently he gave me that field. At least that's what his lawyers tell me. And he still keeps it groomed but he never lets Rachel or her grooms ride there either. What I'm saying is that she probably already hates me. No doubt she would have trashed Ginger's sale even if you hadn't come home."

"Really?" Cassie tilted her head. She wanted to believe that. Hated to think her presence had hurt her grandfather. But the Sutherlands were a powerful family, and she definitely had a history with them.

Gramps gave a confident nod. "Rachel made Santiago switch horses before she even knew you were home."

A slab of guilt lifted from her shoulders. Gramps always had a way of making her feel better. After her parents' deaths, he'd shown up at the hospital, scooped her into his arms and asked if she wanted to meet his ponies. She'd been sad and scared and bewildered, numbed by the fire that had taken away her parents and everything she'd ever known. She'd barely been able to speak, let alone answer any questions. And even though he was technically only a distant relative, he'd taken her home and carved out a place for her in his life—a life that up to then had been devoted to horses.

At first she'd thought him gruff and rather imposing. He was always working with horses, of all shapes and sizes, and he could teach them to do just about anything. Sometimes he'd train a balky animal to jump, or a hunter to stop bucking, but what she remembered most was how he helped riders better enjoy their animals.

Alex's father often brought over his big hunt horses, dropping off Alex in the process. "Can my son stay here for an hour or two? Just while I run down the road? Maybe you can fit in a riding lesson or something."

She hadn't known then where Mr. Sutherland went but Alex was always around a lot longer than an hour. At first she'd been intimidated by the haughty boy perched on the top rail of the round pen. He was four years older than her, handsome, and tall for his age. And he wore real riding clothes, not jeans like her and Gramps. His black leather boots had always been spotless.

When she first came, he'd ignored her, speaking only to Gramps. Asking questions like how to get his horse to stop bucking and what to do when a runaway galloped past the fox hounds and wouldn't stop. But one day she'd been struggling with a bucket of water, and he slid down from the rail and helped her carry it into the barn.

"Where's your groom?" he asked, frowning at the water sloshed on her jeans.

She hadn't even known what a groom was, other than

that was the word Gramps used when he told her to brush a horse. "Never mind," Alex had said quickly. But after that he always carried the water and even helped her clean the stalls.

Gramps had chuckled and said Alex was a paying customer and really shouldn't be doing all her chores. But then added that it was good for kids, even a Sutherland, to learn proper horsemanship.

Gramps used the word 'horsemanship' a lot and by the time she was eight, she could bandage and braid as well as any Sutherland groom. She could also stick like a burr to most horses. Both she and Alex soaked up Gramps' teachings.

She only remembered Alex ever questioning Gramps' decisions once. Someone had brought in a big chestnut gelding with a nasty habit of bolting. She and Alex were riding in the south field and that horse had taken off at a breakneck gallop, then dropped his shoulder and dumped her on the ground, leaving her bruised and gasping for breath.

At first Alex's concerned face had looked blurry. "I'm all r-right," she'd managed, more embarrassed than anything. He'd looked so angry and she'd been afraid he wouldn't want to ride with her anymore if she couldn't keep up.

But Alex had marched right up to her grandfather. "Sir," he said, "I don't think it's right to make Cassie ride your rough stock."

"I don't make her," Gramps said. "She wants to. And where do you think that horse will end up if we can't teach him to stop bolting? Most folks can't afford readymade horses. And this is our livelihood." His face had turned all red and he jammed his finger into Alex's chest, and that was when she first noticed that Alex was taller than Gramps.

Usually Alex nodded at everything Gramps said, but that day he just folded his arms and looked stubborn. "Dad and his friends are into polo now. And I'll be starting lessons this summer so I need my horses in shape. Cassie can work for me."

"But she doesn't know anything about polo," Gramps said. "I don't either. So I can't even help her."

"I'll teach her. I'll teach you both everything I learn."

And Alex had. He'd been a wonderful mentor. His father had flown in high-priced instructors from England and Argentina, and Alex had faithfully relayed the basics of every lesson to her and Gramps. Even when he'd been on the college team with Rachel, he'd passed on playing tips.

She jerked her head away from the clubhouse windows. They were in there now, watching and smirking. Well, they deserved each other. Rachel was nothing more than a vindictive horse abuser and Alex didn't care enough to step outside and say hello.

And it no longer mattered that he'd broken her heart. And been the reason she left Gramps and the home she cherished. Right now she just wanted to get her grandfather away from these entitled snobs and move Ginger back to their safe little barn. Before Rachel had time to take another stab at their innocent horse.

CHAPTER SIX

Alex watched Grace take another dainty bite of pizza, swallow, then carefully wipe her spotless mouth with a napkin. "I like it best with lots of cheese, don't you?" she asked.

He nodded, aching at her too-careful manners. "I used to eat pizza every Saturday night," he said. "There was a place on the south road that loaded it with so much mozzarella that the cheese stuck to the top of the box."

"You had pizza every week?" Grace's eyes widened. "Didn't that make you fat?"

Her horror was so comical he grinned. "We rode horses all day. So we were more scrawny than fat."

Although he remembered returning from his third year at college and being shocked at the way Cassie filled out her T-shirt. He hadn't been able to stop staring and resented the way her new boyfriend ogled her curves. He'd dropped by, hoping to go for a relaxing brook ride, but instead had jumped back in his Jag, muttering that he had to get back to studying for finals.

Fortunately Grace was still a kid. It had been bad enough seeing all the boys hanging around Cassie, pushing each other aside in their efforts to impress. Her grandfather had barely noticed, but that man was oblivious to anything but horses.

"Mom won't go to any restaurants on the south road," Grace said, yanking back his attention. "She says that's where the poor people hang out. And drug dealers and prostitutes."

He almost choked. Hadn't imagined Grace even knew what a prostitute was. And now he was the one to pick up a napkin and unnecessarily wipe his mouth. "What is a prostitute?" he asked, studying her face.

"You know." She gave a disinterested shrug. "People who sell sex for money. Mom said your father went there all the time. And that he was really mean and left you alone at some dumpy barn."

"I wasn't alone. I was with the trainer I told you about, Mr. Edwards."

"The man who taught you to ride?" Grace perked up. "The one who said to always take care of your horse first?"

"That's right."

"Maybe Mom should have taken those lessons too," Grace said. "But I like looking after the horses for her…and I know she appreciates it."

"Sure she does," Alex said. But he doubted Rachel cared that Grace helped the grooms look after the polo ponies. She probably hadn't noticed that their daughter could expertly bandage a horse in minutes and even mixed up her own concoctions of ointments and liniments. Grace was always grasping at straws, struggling to earn her mother's approval. It made him ache.

He balled up his napkin and lobbed it into the trash can. At least she had a mother. And he could compensate for Rachel's shortcomings. He knew from the moment she gleefully announced her pregnancy that shared custody would never be an option. He didn't trust her to look after a cat, let alone a child. But that was okay. As long as Grace was happy, he could be content.

"Do you think Smokey would eat this?" Grace held up a piece of pepperoni tangled in a wad of cheese. "I'm worried she's getting thin. I think the kittens are making her tired. This morning I left some lobster and she didn't even eat it."

Grace was so kind, so concerned, and he couldn't resist reaching over and giving her a hug. "I'll call the vet and have her drop off some special cat food. The kittens are almost ready to leave for new homes anyway."

"Except for Socks," Grace said. "She's the runt and needs more attention. And you promised I could keep one."

"Yes, but remember, she's a barn cat."

"I know," Grace said. "We need the cats in the barn to catch mice." But her eyes sparkled and he suspected the kitten would be firmly ensconced in the poolhouse by the end of the month. It wouldn't be surprising if Grace grew up to become a vet. When he said she could keep one kitten, she'd chosen the tiny female that had almost died. They'd sat up several sleepless nights supplementing milk with a dropper. Now the kitten was healthy and almost as big as her brothers and sisters.

It would have been easy to ask a groom to feed the kitten. But Grace loved having animals to doctor. Maybe he'd been over-zealous about developing her respect for animals. He certainly hadn't been brought up that way. If not for Jake Edwards' teachings, he would have been oblivious, tossing his reins to a waiting groom as if the horse was a disposable machine. His old man had done him a service by dropping him off at Jake's barn, although at the time he'd been resentful.

He hadn't appreciated being stuck all day with a grubby little girl either, but Cassie had turned into one of his favorite playmates. His best friend. And the only woman he'd ever love.

He abruptly scraped back the chair. Didn't want to think about Cassie and her beautiful heart-shaped face, or to remember the hurt in her expressive eyes. Hurt he'd put there.

He yanked some cheese from the top of the remaining pizza and pressed the box shut. "Feed this to Smokey," he said. "Then we can go back to the poolhouse."

"Have you forgotten?" Grace blinked in dismay. "I can't go to bed until the horses are home from the Club. You know I always check on Mom's horses when she can't do it herself."

Rachel never checked on her polo ponies, he thought grimly. She had the grooms do that. Sometimes she acted like the spoiled rich kid and Grace more like the responsible one. Like Cassie. And he needed to cut out any more distracting thoughts about *her*.

"You're right," he said, rising and checking his watch. "The trailers will be back soon. Better get your bandages ready. Soon it'll be a zoo."

Rachel sent a minimum of thirty ponies to every game so it took three huge trailers to ship them to the Polo Club. Each of the four players on her team rode a different horse for each chukka, although high-goal players like Santiago sometimes switched ponies in the middle of a chukka. That still left some spare horses, in case of injury. Anyway, he'd stopped paying attention. As long as Rachel was winning, she was nicer to Grace. That was all that mattered.

Grace hurried to her tack box, all arms and legs and excited energy. "I have some tiger-striped bandages for the new horse," she said. "And a cooler to match. She's well-trained and never pulls when she's tied. They even let me braid her tail this morning."

"That's great." He forced a smile, waiting as she pulled out her pink backpack and rummaged for her wraps. Most of the ponies were obedient, used to being shipped and tied for long hours. And Rachel had the grooms so terrified they would never let Grace work around the more rambunctious animals. So he shouldn't agonize about his daughter standing behind a thousand-pound horse, trying up a tail so it wouldn't interfere with a swinging mallet.

But his unease wouldn't go away. He'd seen people kicked in the head before, and he hated to think of Grace's precious face being slammed by a powerful horse wearing steel shoes. "Maybe you should leave the tails to the grooms," he said. "Especially on polo days."

She pressed a bandage to her chest, eyes wide with dismay. "Don't you think I'm good enough? Is it because of last month? When the knot came out and Mom missed her shot because of me?"

He shook his head. It hadn't been a loose tail that tangled up Rachel's mallet, although she'd blamed Grace for her blunder. "You can braid a tail just great," he said gently. "But sometimes horses kick. Even quiet ones. They know they're going to play polo so they can be excited, easily startled. So maybe you should work around the front legs and skip the back. Just until you're a bit older."

Grace still stared with a mixture of hurt and resentment. He knew he was being over-protective, always on guard against Rachel and anything else that might harm Grace. It would have been easier to watch out for her if she hadn't stopped riding with him. Now her sole interest was to hang out with the grooms and look after horses from the ground and, despite Santiago's assurances, most of the animals seemed a little too spirited.

But Grace wanted to help—needed to feel in control of something—and didn't appreciate his hovering. Besides, he'd always stressed that horses give everything to their riders and it was important to pay it back with good care. She was just trying to do what was right. And she was forever searching for ways to please her mother.

"I have to wrap the back legs too," Grace said, her mouth set in a stubborn line. "Mom expects it. She likes it when I help the grooms."

Voices sounded from the far end of the aisle as tired horses clopped into the barn. Grace shot him a defiant look, clutched her grooming kit to her chest, then rushed out of the tack room. For a moment, her fierce expression reminded him of Cassie when she was that age, determined to do the right thing for a horse.

It had been a hot afternoon and he'd been bored tossing rocks in the brook, waiting for his father to return from his latest mistress. He'd tried to coax Cassie into swimming with him but she'd insisted on lugging extra water to all the horses. At first he thought she was trying to impress her grandfather but it hadn't been that at all. She simply couldn't relax until the horses were tended to first.

He'd helped of course, complaining the entire time, but he'd learned a lesson that day. Taught to him by a little girl who could barely carry a bucket of water without spilling it on her jeans. And Cassie had turned out okay. More than okay.

He sighed and followed Grace toward the front of the barn. He didn't know why he was thinking of Cassie so much lately. That door was closed, and it was one that couldn't be re-opened.

CHAPTER SEVEN

"Poor thing." Grace wiped the mare's bloody sides, her hands shaking with dismay. "Mom must have lost her balance. And when she was trying to stay on, her spurs cut Ginger. Don't you think, Dad?"

"That's probably what happened," Alex said, working hard to conceal his anger. Rachel wasn't a great rider but she was competent. It had been years since he'd seen spur marks on her horses, not since they played together on the college team. Back when he'd been blinded by her beauty, her easy availability—and he'd just been killing time waiting for Cassie to grow up.

"We'll help the mare heal," he said. "She can't be ridden for a while. She shouldn't be turned out either. The flies would drive her crazy. She'll need the cuts washed twice a day along with an antiseptic cream."

He motioned at a groom who jotted down his directions on the whiteboard. "And may I put your name on the bottom," the groom asked, "so everyone knows this horse can't be ridden? And that the order came directly from you?"

Alex reached out and scrawled his bold initials beneath the notation. "What's this mare like on the ground?" he asked the groom, keeping his voice low. "Grace wants to look after her. But is she safe enough?"

"Absolutely." The groom gave an emphatic nod. "She's a sweet mare with impeccable ground manners. She only came in three weeks ago but whoever trained her did an excellent job."

Alex gave a relieved nod. "Okay," he said. "Then Grace will be responsible for the mare's care, under my supervision."

The groom made another quick notation, clearly delighted to have one less animal to look after and even more relieved that there'd be no backlash from Rachel, not with Alex's initials authorizing the change.

Alex turned back to the horse tied in the aisle. The mare would be fine but it was odd Rachel had ridden her so harshly. Grace idolized her mother and her polo skills, preferring to believe the spur marks were accidental. However, he suspected the mare had done something to rouse Rachel's anger.

More reason to personally look after the horse and make sure she was treated fairly. Cassie wasn't the only one who'd been affected by her grandfather's teachings. But dammit, he wasn't going to let himself think about *her* anymore.

"This mare's your responsibility now," he said, turning and smiling at Grace. "Four legs and all."

"Really? I can wrap and brush her tail and try out all my ointments?"

"Yes," he said. "You're in charge. At least until she's ready to ride again."

"How long will that be?"

"A couple weeks."

Grace leaped in excitement. "Awesome! I've never had a polo pony to look after, all on my own before. Not without a groom watching." Her expression turned earnest. "And maybe you should buy Mom some different spurs, the blunt kind. So this won't happen again, you know, in case she loses her balance."

"Good idea," he said. But he really intended to sit Rachel down and warn that there'd be no more polo team if she left a horse with bloody sides again. It was impossible to erase her mean streak, but as always, he'd do whatever was necessary to keep it in check.

◆

Cassie straightened the steering wheel as the trailer bounced over a pothole, almost dragging the small truck into the ditch. There was no reason to speed and risk an accident. Receptions following the big polo games were always elaborate affairs, and she and Ginger would be off the Sutherland Estate long before Rachel and Alex returned home.

Still, it was edging toward eight o'clock, and she wasn't comfortable hauling her grandfather's ancient trailer at night. Even hooking it up to the truck had been a challenge, and the patchwork plug was held together with a piece of frayed electrical tape. But Gramps had been impatient, brushing off her safety concerns.

"Maybe I should pick up Ginger," he'd muttered, "if you're going to make such a big deal out of it."

"No problem," she said cheerfully, refraining from mentioning that he wasn't cleared to drive yet. "A little more tape around the wire and I'll be ready to go."

Besides, it was apparent he was exhausted following the polo game. And though he'd grumbled that he wasn't the least bit tired, he'd already headed for bed by the time she stepped into the truck with the trailer in tow.

She drove slowly along the rutted road, using her side mirror to keep a careful eye on the trailer. Obviously Gramps' money hadn't gone into vehicle maintenance. The truck lights worked but it remained dark behind the trailer. Reflector strips lined the back door though and it was a short drive to the Sutherlands, barely thirty minutes on the back road… Eighteen minutes if mounted and riding cross country.

She and Alex had once completed it in an eight-minute ride that had started with a controlled trot and ended in a competitive heart-pumping gallop. She'd won the race but only because he pulled up. And he'd been on the more dependable horse and most definitely was the better rider. He'd accused her of reckless riding that day, even threatening to tell her grandfather. She knew he wouldn't.

Alex never tattled, even when she foolishly drank some spiked punch at the prom party and called him to drive her home. He pulled over to hold back her hair while she vomited on the floor of his immaculate car. He'd been so gentle with her that night, not so gentle with her inebriated boyfriend.

Alex had come by early the next morning too and cleaned all the stalls, knowing she'd have a hangover but that her grandfather would never notice as long as the chores were done. He'd always been a good friend, her best friend… But now he didn't care enough to step out of the polo club and say hello. Worse, he'd stood back and let his wife hurt Ginger, and trash Gramps.

She spun the dial on the radio, determined to find an upbeat song and not be so affected by Alex and Rachel.

They'd turned into an arrogant power couple who trampled everything, taking what they wanted, whenever they wanted. Then tossed it away like garbage. And she'd allowed them to shape her life for far too long.

She'd been reluctant to face Alex, had avoided her home for years, and it hadn't even been necessary. Because she no longer cared. And it was past time to leave their old memories behind, even the good ones.

CHAPTER EIGHT

"Damn." Cassie shook her head, staring in dismay at the flat tire. Not just flat, but shredded. The trailer had been pulling awkwardly on the last straight stretch but she'd hoped it was her imagination. On the positive side, it was better to have a flat now, when the trailer was empty, rather than when Ginger was loaded. And it wasn't really surprising. The trailer tires were even balder than the truck's.

She strode around the trailer and swung open the side door. No big deal. She'd changed plenty of tires before. And years ago Alex had shoved a trailer-aid jack in the compartment with the tire iron, the kind of ramp that lifts a trailer off the ground, making tire changing a cinch.

"Now that I'm going to college I won't be around to help anymore," he'd said. "And your grandfather doesn't take good care of anything but his horses."

There'd been a hint of disapproval in his voice and she'd punched his arm, hating any criticism of Gramps. Besides, they both knew Alex would have swapped his parents in a heartbeat for her grandfather. Gramps might be absorbed with animals but there was no questioning his love.

Alex's parents had been totally indifferent, worrying

more about their own pursuits than the welfare of their son. Until she was eight, she thought the cook was his mother. However, Alex had been a staunch and loyal friend, as generous with his time as he was with his money.

Fortunate for her, because now she was finally going to use his fancy tire-changing gadget. She'd have this tire switched in five minutes, ten max.

She pulled out the plastic ramp and positioned it on the ground. Then skimmed her phone light over the trailer, searching for the spare. Nothing on the sides. She wheeled and shone the light in every corner of the tack compartment, struggling to accept that it was empty. There was no spare tire.

"Oh, Gramps," she whispered, her shoulders slumping.

He'd always been a little disorganized. But apparently cash was tighter than he pretended, too tight to even invest in a spare tire. And though she was struggling to save for his retirement, he refused to discuss finances, brushing away all offers of help. "Everything is fine," he said every Sunday night when she called. It hadn't been financial help he wanted, but her company. And she hadn't been able to give that. Was physically sick at the thought of seeing Alex, Rachel—and their child—riding and laughing in her backyard.

But she shouldn't have stayed away. Apparently Alex didn't even use the south field. More importantly she shouldn't have taken nine years to stop caring.

She dumped the tire iron and ramp back into the compartment and slammed the door. Tomorrow, bright and early, she'd go into town and buy a replacement tire. For now, she'd unhook the trailer, drive home and come back in the morning to pick up Ginger.

It was a quiet road. The trailer would be fine parked on the shoulder of the road. But a concerned voice kept niggling at her brain. *Ginger might not be.*

Rachel had already demonstrated her vindictiveness. And by the time the reception ended, all the grooms would have returned to their quarters. The stable would be empty. Then Rachel could do anything to Ginger. Clearly Santiago wouldn't stop her. Or Alex. So it was critical to move the mare out of their barn tonight, even it meant a bit of a walk.

Cassie moved around the truck and locked the doors. Leading the mare cross country would be a bit of a hike but it was a familiar route. And she was very close to the Sutherland Estate. Lights flickered over the tree tops, marking the servants' gate. She'd have Ginger home well before midnight, and Gramps wouldn't have to worry about his mare a day longer.

The grooms might be surprised when she showed up on foot, but they couldn't stop her from walking off in the night with her grandfather's horse. Nobody could.

Ten minutes later, she trudged through the unlocked servants' entrance. She didn't need the signs or the ornamental lights to know the barn area was another quarter mile beyond the main house. To the left of the tennis courts and behind the five-bedroom poolhouse. She couldn't resist a nostalgic peek at the Sutherland mansion. She knew the house well, had explored almost every room and spent considerable time watching training videos with Alex. But only when his parents were away, which was almost always.

There were no cars in front of the stately entrance but that didn't mean anything. The ten-car garage was cavernous. Besides, he and Rachel probably hadn't driven themselves to the reception. They would have taken a chauffeured limo, so they could drink and socialize and talk about their expensive polo ponies. And maybe even snicker at Gramps.

She jerked her head away from the house and continued along the long walkway. She'd never really known Rachel. They'd met the first summer Cassie worked as a groom for the Sutherlands. Alex had arranged it and she'd been over the moon with gratitude. Being paid to ride and look after polo ponies was a dream job.

She'd been sixteen the day Alex had driven up to the barn in his newest convertible, Rachel beside him, her long blond hair tied back with an elegant scarf. The older girl was clearly upper crust and they looked perfect together. Alex's parents had even deigned to stay around that evening, and Cassie told herself she was happy for him because while Alex always had a string of eager girlfriends, none had ever accompanied him home from college before.

"Cass, would you please saddle Fritz for Rachel," Alex had said.

It was then the tightness started in her chest. Because even though Alex owned Fritz, no one ever rode him but Cassie. "Don't worry," he said. "Rachel plays with me on the collegiate team. She's been riding horses all her life."

He grinned and rumpled Cassie's hair, and Rachel's eyes had narrowed. There'd been something dark and spiteful in their depths. And Cassie decided maybe his new girlfriend wasn't so beautiful after all. But that summer she didn't see Rachel again. Cassie and Alex both played at the Ponhook Club while Rachel was busy with a team in New York. And life had been wonderful.

She and Alex had both been working toward attaining a higher polo ranking. Players were ranked from a minus two to plus ten. Cassie had been a minus one goal handicap and Alex was an amazing plus four. They practiced their passing and shots at the Club as well as on the south field, and their teamwork had never been better. She enjoyed a string of four good polo ponies. Two were off-the-track Thoroughbreds, retrained by Gramps, and the other two polo ponies, Fritz and Suzy, were owned by Alex. Best of all, she earned a generous paycheck.

"You're paying me too much," she'd said to Alex. "You know I'd ride for pizza."

He just grinned and slid another slice of Saturday night pizza onto her plate. "You double as my groom and exercise rider and you're an intuitive player. You're the real deal." He'd affectionately tousled her hair. "Plus a girl like you doesn't eat much."

He never threw out compliments easily. That same morning he'd chewed her out for trying a dangerous shot. But somehow his words left her unsatisfied—just another demonstration of how he treated her like she was still a kid, even though her current boyfriend was almost his age.

"I wish you wouldn't ruffle my hair like that," she'd muttered. "I don't like it."

"Sorry, Cass," he said, his expression unreadable. "I'll stop." And he never touched her hair again. Until—

Dammit, no. She wasn't going there. Wasn't going to think about his hands, his mouth, how their bodies had fit together so beautifully. It was easier to remember her tears and those sleepless nights she had to jam the pillow over her face so Gramps wouldn't hear her sobs.

Everyone at the polo club had toasted Alex and Rachel's

engagement, raving about how they were the perfect couple. A high-society family from New York with the vaunted Sutherlands of Virginia. The ideal match. Cassie had been miserable. Three weeks later, she stuffed her boots and jeans into her backpack and headed to West Virginia to work at a spa facility for horses.

Gramps had been sad she was moving but also impressed she landed such a job. "That's an excellent establishment," he'd admitted. "And you've always wanted a career with horses. It's a good move for you." He hadn't seemed to realize why she was leaving. And though she never regretted her employment there—it had led to her job training horses for the films— she did regret letting Alex and Rachel drive her away.

But this situation was different. She was older and wiser now. Tougher too. And this time she wasn't going to let anybody stop her from taking proper care of Gramps. Or his horse.

CHAPTER NINE

Cassie trudged past the staff quarters. Both grooms and house staff lived in the tasteful apartments, each with more floor space than Gramps' bungalow. No one stepped out to question her presence although she caught subdued voices and the flicker of television screens as they cut the night.

Alex's ancestors had built their first house on this spot and though it had since been remodeled for staff, she'd seen paintings of the original home in a place of honor above the staircase, alongside countless black and white photos of the first Sutherland owned railway. That early enterprise had been the foundation of Sutherland Holdings, which had equity interests in corporations worldwide.

His privileged background had never been more apparent but she'd spent a lot of time on his family estate and fortunately knew all the short cuts. Alex had always preferred to use the servants' entrance rather than the security-coded front gate. And if she slipped around the back of the horse path and across the little wooden bridge, she'd save another few minutes of walking.

It was obvious she was close when the path changed to nonslip rubberized bricks, specially designed for equine safety. The Sutherlands were as passionate about their horses as they were about their family history.

A row of silver trailers gleamed beneath the moonlight. They were much bigger than Gramps' two-horse budget trailer and far more luxurious, with accommodations for both horses and people. She'd always appreciated the little fridge and bunks. Had loved accompanying the horses to each polo match, delighted to be working for the respected Sutherland family. Those had been the happiest years of her life.

Game day routine was imprinted in her mind. Rush over from Gramps before sunup, feed and load the horses, then drive over to the polo club. She was the only groom who played on Alex's team, and it had been his tutelage and generosity that made it possible.

She remembered the day he'd invited her to join the team. That spring they had spent long, hot hours in the south field, practicing plays he'd learned in college and conditioning the horses. She'd gone from retrieving his balls to returning his passes, matching him stride for stride on the field.

They'd been eating pizza on her grandfather's verandah when Alex casually made the announcement. "I'm hiring an extra groom for the game this weekend," he said. "That will free you up to play with me."

At first she'd only gaped. She knew there was an opening on the Sutherland team since his father had chosen to play in Europe, but members were either professional players or else hailed from an established polo family. Besides, everyone viewed her as a groom, or at best, a practice player. She didn't even own four polo ponies.

"You can ride Fritz and Suzy," Alex had said, grinning. "And your grandfather's two Thoroughbreds will be okay. If they don't work out, I'll pick you up a few more."

"So this isn't just one game?"

"No." His expression turned serious. "I want you long term."

He seemed to be studying her reaction but all she could think about were the blue-blooded Club members who too often felt entitled, and would likely give up their first born to play on the Sutherland team.

"You don't think anyone will mind?" she'd asked slowly.

"You'll have everyone's support," he told her. And she knew it had been an unnecessary question. Alex was determined to make polo more open. And he might poke fun at her, but he never let anyone else tease. Once at a horse show, he'd punched a boy much older than him for ridiculing her cast-off Thoroughbred.

Reassured, she leaped from the chair, hugged his neck and then rushed out to the barn to tell her grandfather.

She hadn't been much help to Gramps those three summers following high school. It had been exhausting, working as well as competing. And it didn't stop after the games. The tired horses always needed to be bathed and fed, their legs wrapped, and any injuries tended. Back then, Alex had helped, working alongside her until all the animals were tucked in their stalls for the night. Her grandfather's Thoroughbreds, purchased at rummage-sale prices, had been assigned spacious stalls and given star treatment, just like the costly Sutherland horses.

Unfortunately, times had changed and it was clear Ginger didn't rate that sort of care now. Cassie's stride turned jerky. It was infuriating that Rachel could spur a willing mount around the field and then order the helpless horse to be tied beneath the hot sun. To a stinky toilet! And not one person had protested.

Grooms were usually animal lovers, devoted to their charges, but obviously they were terrified of their employer. Worse, Alex hadn't lifted a finger to stop her. He was no longer the wonderful man she'd known, and he and Rachel deserved each other.

Her hands fisted and she burst through the wide barn door, into the polished alleyway framed with stalls crafted from furniture-grade red oak. She doubted Ginger would be here. The mare was probably stuck outside in a paddock somewhere, providing a meal for blood-sucking mosquitoes. There were no grooms in sight to ask, but the aisle was L-shaped, with the office at the back. Cassie promised herself she'd stay calm for Gramps' sake, but if they'd mistreated his horse again it would be difficult to ignore.

She swept around the corner, prepared to do battle. And immediately spotted Ginger.

The mare wasn't being abused. In fact, she was in crossties in the aisle, eating hay from a wheelbarrow thoughtfully placed within reach. A young girl crooned a lullaby while she gently applied ointment to Ginger's ribs.

Ginger flicked an ear, curiously eyeing Cassie, but continued munching at the alfalfa.

The girl glanced up. "I thought everyone was gone. And there was no place to tie a hay net. That's why I put the wheelbarrow there. It's okay, isn't it?" Her tone was a childish mixture of defensiveness and uncertainty.

"Sure," Cassie said. "I've done that before. Horses

appreciate being able to eat after a long day."

The girl gave a relieved smile and continued dabbing blue ointment onto Ginger's cuts. "You don't have to supervise me," she said. "Ginger is well behaved. And I'm allowed to look after her by myself."

Clearly she mistook Cassie for a groom. There were so many Sutherland workers nobody could remember all their faces. And the barn was crammed with sleek horses, every stall full. It seemed Alex and Rachel owned enough polo ponies to field two teams, and the amount of money invested in horseflesh was so gross it almost made Cassie ill.

"Ginger's stall is at the end across from the office," the girl went on. "It has a fan that will keep flies away even if she rubs off the ointment. And tomorrow I'll put on a sheet and take her out for some grass. We don't think she should be turned out though. Do you?"

"No," Cassie said slowly. "Probably not. The flies are pretty bad this time of year." Her fingers uncurled from her fists, her anger fizzling. She'd been prepared to fight every groom on the Sutherland payroll, but this girl clearly intended to take good care of the mare. As if she already had a relationship with the horse…and maybe she'd know when those spur marks had really occurred.

"Did you put anything on her cuts this morning?" Cassie asked, feeling a bit guilty for interrogating someone so young. "Before she went on the trailer?"

"No," the girl said. "Ginger was fine then. This happened at the polo game."

Ah-ha! So it was Rachel. And now Gramps would have proof. Cassie hid her triumph, slid her phone from her pocket and discreetly pressed the Record button. "So you saw Ginger this morning," she repeated. "And she had no marks? No scars or cuts of any kind?"

"I didn't see her this morning," the girl said, "but I saw her last night. I helped give her a bath. I feel bad she's cut now but at least I get to look after her. Most of the polo ponies are too jumpy. The last time a horse was quiet enough for me to handle was over a month ago." She gave Ginger a kiss on her nose then fluffed up the hay in the wheelbarrow so the mare could reach the best pieces.

It sounded like this girl didn't ride. Just enjoyed looking after them on the ground. But she'd taken care of the mare, and now Cassie had proof that Ginger was fine before being entrusted to Santiago. Gramps could show the committee that it definitely hadn't been him who cut up Ginger's sides.

She gave a sigh of relief and held her phone out a little further. "So you're saying the horse was unmarked last night. That her rider did this today, not the original trainer? You're sure of that?"

"Positive. But Mom didn't mean it. She really didn't."

Cassie froze, her hand stuck midair. She stared at Alex and Rachel's daughter, barely able to breathe. Then her skin prickled in an old familiar sensation, and she knew he was behind her.

She pulled in a gulp of air, lowered her phone and turned.

"Hello, Cassie," Alex said. His face was the same, his handsome features still perfectly chiseled, but his shoulders looked bigger, more formidable. And though his tone was polite, his mouth was hard, almost as hard as his ice-blue eyes. "Please tell me why you're recording my daughter?"

CHAPTER TEN

Cassie had imagined countless reunions with Alex over the years. In some of her dreams, he and Rachel had snickered at her juvenile infatuation. In the best ones he dropped to his knees, confessing that he had never stopped loving her and wished he'd never married Rachel. But she'd never anticipated his chilly glare, the kind she'd seen him use on others who'd displeased him. Certainly never on her.

She straightened her spine. "Good to see you too, Alex," she said.

He just stared, his arms crossed. She thought the side of his mouth twitched but she could have imagined it. The overhead lights shadowed his profile but regrettably he was just as gorgeous as ever. However, all he did was stare.

"Gramps had a heart attack," she added. "I came back to help him."

"Sorry to hear that. But that's not what I asked." He sounded genuinely sorry but his big arms remained crossed and he was still looking at her hand... No, at her phone.

She quickly tucked the offending phone back in her pocket. Obviously he was annoyed about the recording but no way was she giving it up. That might be the only thing that could salvage her grandfather's reputation.

"I'm here to pick up Ginger," she said, amazed at the calmness of her voice. "Santiago was supposed to ride her. No one else. So it was decided we should take her home."

"Ginger is your horse?" And now he looked surprised. An odd expression crossed his face, one almost of resignation. Then his expression shuttered. He gave a polite dip of his head. "We'll find some shipping bandages and help you load her."

"But, Dad!" the girl behind them said. "Ginger can't leave. I'm supposed to look after her."

"This is Grace." Alex's entire manner softened when he turned toward his daughter. "Cassie's grandfather was my old trainer."

He didn't say they'd been childhood friends or that they'd ridden together every day for ten years. Cassie didn't expect him to admit they had dated. But he certainly trivialized their relationship, and even though she was prepared for it, his words hurt.

"Couldn't Ginger stay?" Grace asked, staring at Cassie with imploring eyes. "Please, just until she's better? I'll take good care of her. Since it's Mom's fault I really should be the one to look after her."

Cassie's hand flattened over the phone in her pocket. She wished she had *that* statement recorded on her phone. But the raw appeal in the girl's voice yanked at her heartstrings. She spent a lot of time with children on the movie sets and horse-crazy girls were her favorite. And she knew how much it hurt to watch a horse leave. "Well—"

"No," Alex said, his voice clipped. "It's best if Ginger

goes home now. Tonight."

Cassie slowly closed her mouth. Clearly he didn't want her around. Or Ginger. Which was fine because she didn't want her grandfather's horse here either. And she shouldn't have let herself be softened by foolish empathy for his daughter.

"Grab some shipping bandages," Alex said to Grace, gesturing toward the tack room.

"Thanks," Cassie said, her voice just as clipped. "But bandages aren't necessary. I had a flat so I'm leading Ginger home."

Grace tilted her head in confusion then placed a protective hand on Ginger's neck. "But how far away do you live? I didn't know there were other stables on our road. And I think Ginger is too tired to walk."

"We're not on your road," Cassie said gently, appreciating the girl's concern for the mare. "But it's not so far if I cut across the back fields. She'll be fine."

"It's dark though," Grace said. "And strange people live there. That's why Mom never rides in the south field. It's not a nice place."

"It's okay." A flush warmed Cassie's face and she didn't look at Alex. "I know the area well."

She unclipped Ginger from the cross ties and attached her lead line, outwardly poised but intent on keeping her hand from shaking. Alex really had changed. She'd told herself that maybe he hadn't seen her at the polo game — and clearly he hadn't known that Ginger belonged to Gramps — but there was no question, he definitely wanted them both gone. Tonight. The old Alex would have worried about her walking off in the dark. This new Alex was silent, just watching her with hooded eyes.

"But isn't it dangerous to lead a horse alone at night?" Grace persisted.

"Not if I'm careful," Cassie said.

"But, Dad!" Grace wheeled toward her father. "Didn't you always say it was more dangerous at night? Especially if a horse is alone?"

"Yes," Alex said, his voice resigned. "So we'll walk across the field and give them some company."

Cassie's chest flared with panic. She did *not* want to walk across their old playground with Alex and his daughter. "That's not necessary," she said.

"But I think it is," Alex said. And he gave her that regal Sutherland look, a look perfected over centuries by a family accustomed to looking out for the welfare of their animals, their servants, their boardrooms…and their neighbors. She knew from experience it was useless to argue. But it was just as apparent he was walking her home, not out of affection but because of a deep-rooted chivalry, and also his desire to appease Grace.

◆

Stars dotted the sky and a fat white moon illuminated the open fields. Cassie squeezed Ginger's lead rope tighter against her palm, keeping the mare beside her at a measured walk. It was easy enough to see and the rolling ground was devoid of holes. But her legs felt awkward and it was hard to concentrate on Grace's tentative questions. She was far too aware of Alex's imposing figure, striding tall and silent on the other side of his daughter.

Cassie nodded again, fighting to keep her words from sounding stilted. "Yes, I used to live around here. My grandfather gave your dad some riding lessons."

"Did you play polo too?" Grace asked.

"A little," Cassie said. "Not as well as your parents though."

"But Dad doesn't play polo. Only Mom."

She couldn't help it. Her head jerked sideways. Alex had barely spoken since they left the barn, since he'd insisted on walking her home. Moonlight reflected on his face. He was staring straight ahead, not smiling but not frowning either.

This was totally weird. He had all those polo ponies in the barn—and he didn't play?

"Well," she said slowly, "he used to be a good player, the best in this area."

"Santiago is the best now," Grace said. "Mom says Dad can't even remember how to swing a mallet."

The idea was so ludicrous Cassie almost laughed. Alex was a superb athlete, rarely missing a shot. He certainly remembered how to swing a mallet. Yet Grace was almost snickering at his skill. Obviously she'd never seen him play. Why had he given up a sport he loved? Polo was the one thing he'd shared with his dad. That and making money were the only two things that had ever earned his father's approval.

Alex had practiced long hours in order to make the Sutherland team. He even helped Cassie with barn chores so she'd have more time to hit balls with him. Most nights he didn't leave Gramps' house until after dark, and he was always quizzing her grandfather about horse psychology, keen to learn why some animals were natural polo ponies while others preferred a different line of work.

"Hitting balls isn't the only thing to do with a horse," Alex said, as if reading her mind. "Cassie works with them in the movie industry."

She glanced sideways again, surprised he even knew where she worked. She hadn't kept in touch with old acquaintances and her grandfather said he hadn't spoken to Alex in years. Alex wasn't looking at her though. He was smiling down at Grace, his expression so tender it was obvious he doted on his daughter. And something tightened in Cassie's chest.

"The movies?" Grace gave an excited skip and turned toward Cassie. "Really? So you work with horses on the ground? You don't have to ride?"

"Not usually," Cassie said, clearing her throat. "But I'm just an assistant, more of a wrangler. My boss is the head trainer."

"What sort of things does he teach them?"

"Whatever the movie needs. Roll over, play dead or even to jump through fire. Once he had a movie about a famous racehorse and needed to teach a Thoroughbred to leap into a swimming pool."

"Sweet." Grace's eyes glowed. "I'd love to do something like that."

Her enthusiasm was so genuine Cassie's mouth lifted in a smile. A wrangler's job was hard work and definitely not prestigious. Grace didn't seem to realize she'd never need a job like that. Not with the Sutherland money.

"When Cassie was your age," Alex said, "she trained her grandfather's horses to stand in the brook so we could jump off their backs."

Cassie's smile deepened. She remembered every animal she'd ever trained. Unfortunately it seemed that whenever she finally had a horse willing to stand still while they climbed over its slippery back, her grandfather sold the horse. It had been upsetting. Alex had always taken her home and cheered her up by letting her leap off his Olympic-sized diving board.

"Jumping in a brook sounds like fun," Grace said, bouncing with delight.

"It was," Alex said. His voice shifted and she felt his appraisal. Luckily it was night and she was busy leading Ginger and had an excuse to avoid his eyes. She never could hide her feelings from him, and his gaze seemed even more perceptive now.

"Can you teach me how to train a horse to stand in a brook?" Grace asked.

"No!" Both she and Alex spoke at the same time, their voices raised in shared horror. She understood her panic although his quick protest was surprising. And hurtful.

"Cassie is just home to see her grandfather," Alex went on, his voice level again. "She doesn't have much time."

Perhaps she'd mistaken the horror in his voice. And she definitely didn't plan on spending any more time with Grace, no matter that Alex's daughter was so likeable. Clearly they both agreed on that.

"I'm here to help my grandfather sell his horses," she said lightly. "And everything is really rushed right now."

"I understand." Grace's tone was polite but her obvious disappointment left Cassie feeling torn.

"The most important thing," she said, smiling down at Grace, "is to start with a patient horse. One who doesn't mind being away from his friends. And it helps if they have a long mane and a broad back."

Grace gave an enthusiastic nod. "I'll remember that. And would it help if I hung a feedbag over the horse's nose, so he can eat at the same time?"

"No. That would be dangerous. Water might get in the

bag and the horse could drown. And you don't want to be trying this with your parents' polo ponies." She gripped Ginger's lead line a little tighter. No doubt, Alex and Rachel wouldn't want their fancy horses standing in a brook all day.

"Yes." Grace's voice dulled. "All our polo ponies have shaved manes. And I wouldn't be able to do it anyway. I'm not good at anything except grooming and bandaging."

Cassie stiffened. What a horrible way to feel. And she didn't understand why this girl didn't own a quiet pony, something to build up her confidence. She looked over Grace's head at Alex, and once again he seemed to pick up on her thoughts. He gave his head a little shake and for a moment the powerful Alex Sutherland looked almost helpless.

"You sure did a good job with Ginger's cuts today," Cassie said, keeping her voice bright.

"I made the ointment myself," Grace said. "It works really well. I can come over and put some on Ginger tomorrow if you'd like." Moonlight revealed the hopeful expression on her upturned face. "Since you're busy with your grandfather and might want help?"

"No, Grace," Alex said, his voice gentle but firm. He turned to Cassie. "There's a boggy section just ahead. Pass me your phone and I'll check the ground."

Cassie halted Ginger and gave him her phone. They were entering the back section of the south field. The grass looked level and she couldn't remember this area ever being soft but she'd been away a long time. Another few minutes and she and Ginger would be home.

Home. She blew out a disbelieving sigh. It was

wonderful to be back, even if the polo game hadn't gone according to plan. And it hadn't been so awful walking with Alex and Grace. Obviously he didn't want her seeing his daughter again, but they were in agreement on that. And it was rather comforting he'd insisted on walking her home. A nice note for their final good-bye.

Ginger pawed at the ground, her ears pinned on the tree-lined path. Clearly she knew they were close and was impatient to return to her barn. And Cassie didn't need the light on her phone. There was plenty of moonlight.

"I can see perfectly," she said, holding out her hand for her phone. "We can walk alone the rest of the way. Thanks for the company. It was nice to see you again, and it was great to meet Grace."

Alex still hadn't managed to turn on her light. He was fumbling with her phone. ... No, not fumbling. His deft fingers flew over the screen.

She jerked back, feeling like she'd been sucker punched. Now she realized why he'd insisted on walking her home. It wasn't because of their old friendship at all, or even to satisfy Grace. He'd just wanted a chance to delete the recording. Protecting his wife by erasing Grace's comment that Ginger hadn't been bloody before the game.

"Are you quite finished?" she asked, hating the hurt in her voice that she couldn't hide. And that she still used her birth date as the password.

"Now I am," he said, passing over the phone. "Please give your grandfather my regards."

And even though he'd successfully removed all evidence against Rachel, his voice wasn't triumphant. In fact, he sounded almost regretful.

CHAPTER ELEVEN

Feet shuffled in the kitchen. Cassie shoved aside the sheets and scrambled out of bed. If she didn't hurry, Gramps would feed the horses, and he wouldn't stop with tossing hay and grain. How much did a water bucket weigh anyway? More than he should lift, that was for sure. And then she'd agonize all day, worrying that the exertion might cause another heart attack.

She yanked on a T-shirt and jeans and bolted down the narrow hall.

"Morning, Gramps," she called, catching him just as he was reaching in the closet.

Boots thumped back on the floor and he shot her a sheepish look. "Thought I'd help feed this morning," he said. "And check on Ginger. How did the trailering go last night? Did you see Santiago or that woman?"

That woman.

Cassie shook her head, hoping she could avoid mentioning the flat tire. She was supposed to keep Gramps calm, not worry him with trivial details. From the front of the house, he couldn't see that the truck and trailer weren't parked in their usual spot. Maybe she'd find a spare tire kicking around in the shed and be able to haul the trailer back before he even noticed.

He was too proud to accept her money, and he'd only get defensive if she mentioned his tires needed replacing. It was best not to say anything and simply buy new ones without him knowing.

"No one was at the Sutherland barn except for Alex and his daughter." She pulled out a kitchen chair, encouraging her grandfather to sit. "They were taking good care of Ginger... Alex asked me to say hello."

"Do they have many horses over there? Is their barn full?"

"All forty stalls," she said, marginally relaxing. Gramps was too interested in horses to quiz her about tires, or people. He wasn't going to ask any tough questions about the Sutherlands either. Like if Grace looked like Alex, or if Alex was happy...or if Cassie still loved him.

"Their barn is full of good-looking polo ponies," she said. "Even more than when Alex's dad was alive. And Ginger wasn't outside. She was in a big stall at the office end of the barn."

Cassie walked over to the sink, picked up a washcloth and began scrubbing the spotless counter.

"Alex didn't see us at the polo game," she went on. "He mentioned that he and Grace left early. I don't think he even knew Ginger was your horse." She didn't know why she was babbling. Or why she felt compelled to defend Alex.

"But of course Alex didn't know," Gramps said, his voice matter-of-fact. "Or he wouldn't have let it happen."

She tossed the cloth aside with a sense of relief. Her grandfather preferred horses to humans, but he did understand people. If he still held a high opinion of Alex, then clearly Alex hadn't changed that much. And she wasn't going to upset Gramps by telling him about Grace's recording—the one that had vindicated him—the one Alex had deleted. After all, it was understandable a man would want to help his wife. Especially a protective man like Alex.

She pulled open the cupboard door and rummaged for the coffee. It wasn't healthy to dwell on Alex and Rachel. She just appreciated being home, being able to eat breakfast with Gramps and talk about old horses, and people, and of course, polo.

"I wonder why Alex doesn't play polo anymore," she mused, keeping her back to Gramps. "Especially since his wife still plays. Maybe they're not totally happy…?"

"He stopped playing polo before his daughter was born," Gramps said. "And of course he's not happy. That's why they're divorced."

Her hand froze around the coffee container and she felt the blood draining from her face. It was a relief Gramps couldn't see her expression. "How long have they been divorced?" she managed, her eyes fixed on the cupboard.

"Not sure. Rumors started back when he sold that Thoroughbred stallion of his. Wish I could have bred a mare to that stud. He was a beauty. Alex thought a lot of him. So did his father, and the Sutherlands know their horses—"

"How many years, Gramps?"

"Don't know. Six or seven, I guess."

She wrapped both hands around the coffee tin, trying to stop their shaking. This was worse. Alex had been divorced all that time and hadn't even bothered to let her know. Hadn't cared enough to reach out. While she'd thought about him often, convinced they would have had a future together if it hadn't been for Rachel's untimely pregnancy.

She remembered his quick rejection the previous night when Grace had asked about training lessons. Even now he didn't want to rekindle relations, even as a friend. Her breathing sounded loud, drowning out the sound of the ticking kitchen clock.

Her grandfather was still praising the athleticism of Thoroughbreds and how their competitive nature was important for polo. Usually she appreciated any kind of horse talk with Gramps. But right now, she just wanted to slink back into her room and hide.

She'd totally misjudged Alex's feelings. Had built their friendship up in her mind, letting it overshadow all other relations. No friend had ever matched him, no lover had ever come close to rousing the same passion. She'd avoided him geographically, hadn't once googled his name, but emotionally he'd never left her heart.

She'd been a fool.

She ripped off the lid and dumped in the coffee, too off balance to count the scoops. But it would definitely be strong.

"I'll feed the horses now," she said, jamming the coffee container back into the cupboard and wheeling toward the door. "Be back in twenty minutes to make breakfast. Then we can talk about the best way to help you retire."

She shoved open the screen door and escaped onto the verandah. The sun was just poking over the horizon, the morning air crisp. She'd always loved the start of the day here, knowing there were horses to feed, to ride, to teach. But today she just stared blankly at the barn, dismayed at her numbing sense of loss. Really, life was no different than it had been yesterday so it was ridiculous to feel like this—helpless, hollow, unwanted.

A hungry horse nickered from inside the barn and she gave her head a shake. She had to stay focused. Alex was truly out of her life now, and that was a good thing. It wasn't even his fault. She'd built him up into the perfect man, her soul mate, obsessing about all the thoughtful things he'd done. How he'd always shown her how much he cared.

And maybe he had, once. But that was years ago. Things were different now.

She thumped down the wooden steps and headed toward the barn. At least she was back with her grandfather, home where she'd ached to be for almost a decade. She had to straighten her thoughts though if she were going to be any help to Gramps.

Today she'd ride each horse, except for Ginger, and assess their market value. After that she'd hike down the road and pick up the truck, then find a spare tire and collect the trailer. Hopefully she'd have time to check Internet listings for other clubs. She'd contact them before Rachel had time to spread her poison.

If the four horses didn't sell as polo ponies, their worth would be drastically reduced. Unfortunately every player in this area belonged to the Ponhook Club so she would have to go further afield for buyers.

She trudged around the corner, making a mental to-do list as she walked past the trailer.

Trailer?

She whirled, her eyes widening. Yes, her grandfather's horse trailer was really there, parked in its usual spot beside the barn. And the truck was parked beside it. They weren't sitting on the back road where she'd abandoned them last night. Her body turned so taut it was impossible to move, and she could only stare as if dropped in some twilight zone.

She squeezed her eyes shut. When she opened them, the trailer was still there, still sitting on its regular patch of dried-out grass. She reached out, cautiously touching its metal frame. It was reassuringly solid. And it didn't have a shredded tire. In fact, all four tires were sparkling new, white lines gleaming against the shiny black rubber.

Alex was the only person she knew with enough money and clout to move a locked truck and have four premium trailer tires installed before six am. And he was the only one she'd told about her flat tire. This was the type of thing he used to do for her …before he married Rachel.

But it didn't make sense. And while she was grateful, the gesture left her bewildered. She wanted him out of her head, for good this time. Not filling it with conflicting feelings of frustration and gratitude.

And worse, even a little hope.

CHAPTER TWELVE

"You'd really enjoy working with the film horses," Cassie said. She leaned further over the kitchen table, her eyes on Gramps. "And you'd like my boss, Dan Barrett. He's great with the animals. His training philosophy is a lot like yours."

Her grandfather pushed away his plate, his scowl quick and scornful. "But I wouldn't like living in a trailer, moving around all the time. Different states, different people. Sounds like you're nothing but a nomad."

Cassie flinched. It was an itinerant life. She never was able to memorize the roll of a field, the lay of the land, and the people around her always changed. Some of her jobs weren't even in North America. But she had learned to like it, and so would Gramps. "I have an apartment in L.A.," she said, "so I do have a base. But I like to keep busy."

"I like to keep busy too," her grandfather grumbled. "But here. In one spot. And I like to get up and feed horses, not live in an apartment and wait for a phone call about my next job."

Cassie took a pensive sip of coffee. She hadn't realized he'd been listening so closely during their phone calls. She'd tried to conceal her homesickness. And she was used to that life now. But it was obvious her grandfather wouldn't be happy sharing her apartment, away from the house and barn and the paddocks he'd built. However, it would be awhile before he'd be medically cleared to resume riding, and even then he'd have to slow down. With no pension or savings, a financial buffer was crucial.

If she were to help him remain in his home, she'd have to sell those horses quickly. And it was vital to obtain a good price. But because of Rachel's slander their options would be limited. The Internet was vast and far reaching. It might be possible to train the horses to jump but the animals weren't big enough to make high-level hunters. A polo home would definitely be best—for both the animals and Gramps.

"I'll call my boss," she said. "He recently finished a polo film. Maybe he knows of another one that needs horses. And I'll check with some out-of-state clubs. But first I'll ride the other horses so I know what we have."

"Ginger's the best of the four," her grandfather said. "She'd suit a high-level player. The others are solid, although Tex is a little suspicious of strange things." He dragged a worried hand over his face. "Ginger won't be happy alone in the barn but the old fly sheet is ripped. It'll be a few days before those cuts are healed enough to turn her out."

"Don't worry," Cassie said. "I'll take good care of your horses."

"I know. You always do." His voice turned gruff. "And I'm very glad you moved back."

I'm only back for a few weeks. But there was no point reminding him. She didn't want to add to his worry. Even though he'd only been up a few hours, dark shadows underscored his eyes. "You have a nap," she said. "I'll clean up the breakfast dishes when I come back in."

"I'll lie down for a minute," he said, rising from the chair. "Doubt I'll sleep." His forehead creased as he stared out the window. "Who the hell is that kid sitting by the barn?"

Cassie rose, following his gaze then stiffened at the sight. Grace sat on the ground, arms clasped around her knees. A pink backpack lay by her feet. She looked small and uncertain, but there was an unmistakable look of determination in the set of her shoulders.

"That's Grace," Cassie said. "Alex's daughter." She stepped closer to the window and scanned the driveway, both relieved and disappointed when she didn't see a car. "It's time for me to ride anyway," she said. "See you at lunch."

She pulled on her boots and stepped outside. Grace scrambled to her feet.

"Good morning," the girl called. "I brought some ointment for Ginger. It works great on cuts. And I have a flysheet and some molasses treats, and I was really hoping you'd let me see her."

Grace spoke fast and was clearly nervous, but her concern for Ginger was heartwarming. It was too bad Rachel didn't share a fraction of her daughter's sense of responsibility.

"Of course you can see her," Cassie said. "Did your dad drop you off?"

"No." Grace bent down and scooped up her backpack. "I walked across the fields. It only took twenty-three minutes. I timed it so I could get back in time."

"In time for what?"

"You know." Grace gave a vague shrug. "Before

everyone finishes riding."

She followed Cassie into the barn, still talking about the special ointment she'd made and how the local vet had even bought some bottles.

"This is a really cute barn," Grace said, pausing to catch her breath. "Are those all your ribbons?"

Cassie glanced at the dusty ribbons mounted on the wall. Her grandfather had taken her to a variety of shows, both English and western, depending on the type of horses he was training. "It's good for folks to see a little girl showing a horse," he'd said. "And it helps to have ribbons above the horses' stalls. It adds value."

She hadn't thought about how ribbons would help sell a horse and had simply enjoyed the shows, especially the times when Alex had joined them.

"They're not all mine," she said. "Some of them are your dad's." She gestured at a huge blue ribbon with the silhouette of a horse and rider leaping a fence. She remembered that weekend well. Alex's housekeeper had been sick and his mom had been in Europe. So his father had dumped him off.

"Give him some riding lessons or something," Mr. Sutherland had said, leaning out of his big black car and pressing a wad of bills into her grandfather's hand. "I'll pick the kid up on Sunday night."

At first Alex had been grumpy about having to stay the entire weekend, but Gramps had given him their best horse to ride, and Alex had done so well at the hunter show someone had purchased the gelding on the spot. And then she was the one who was grumpy—not just because she'd been riding that horse for months and then Gramps sold him—but also because Alex was constantly beating her.

However, Alex had been a big help, even Saturday night after the show when everyone was tired and hungry. He'd lugged everything in from the trailer, wrapped all the horses' legs, and also found a hammer and nails so he could hang the ribbons.

"Don't you want to keep your ribbons?" she'd asked. "You won them."

"They mean more to your grandfather," he said, tousling her hair. "I'm glad I could help with the sale though. Did you see that kid's face? He was sure happy with his new horse. I think your grandfather will have enough money to go out for ice cream tonight."

She'd been ten years old and that was the day she realized Gramps didn't sell the horses to be mean. It was how he paid their bills. And that blond kid only wanted to buy the horse because Alex looked so cool, and everyone knew the Sutherlands were great riders. The kid might not have wanted anyone to know that a little girl could ride the horse over jumps too.

"My dad rode horses at shows?" Grace's surprised voice yanked back Cassie's attention.

"Sure," Cassie said. "When he was young. Before he switched to polo." She paused. Grace was staring up at the wall, a wistful expression on her face.

"Do you want your dad's ribbons?" Cassie asked. "You can take them home with you."

"No, thanks. I didn't win them." Grace wrapped her arms around her backpack and turned away. "I'll just groom Ginger while you ride…if that's okay?"

"Sure," Cassie said. She hesitated a moment then headed toward the bay gelding's stall. She'd worked with lots of children on film sets, but she'd never met one who was so polite. Or maybe Grace was just insecure. Whatever, there was something different about her. And it made Cassie want to hang around and try to make the kid relax. Which was a little surprising because she'd been prepared to resent Alex and Rachel's child.

She tacked up Digger, grabbed a helmet and led the gelding outside. She had more important things to worry about, like helping Gramps sell his horses so he didn't work himself into an early grave.

An hour later, she kicked her feet out of the stirrups, leaned forward and patted Digger's sweaty neck. He was a lovely horse, responsive, keen and willing. His turns weren't as crisp as she'd like, but tomorrow they'd go to the south field with a ball and mallet. A lot of horses woke up when they had something to chase. Either way, he'd make a solid polo pony. He wasn't as fiery as Ginger but he'd be great for an intermediate player. As usual, Gramps had done an excellent training job.

"Did you ride looking like that?"

Cassie swiveled in the saddle, surprised to see Grace standing by the barn door. She'd thought the girl would be long gone by now.

"What do you mean?" she asked.

"You ride in jeans?" Grace stepped closer, her eyes wide with horror. "Not breeches? Not real riding clothes?"

"I sure do," Cassie said. Sometimes she added chaps to keep her legs from chafing, but only for strenuous gallops or rough brush rides.

"But Mom says I always have to wear breeches."

"It's good to follow the dress rules of every discipline." Cassie chose her words carefully. "But I work with different horses all day. Both on the ground and in the saddle. So it's more important to be practical."

"You mean when you work around famous movie stars, you still wear jeans?"

Cassie nodded, hiding her amusement. The girl looked aghast at the thought of appearing in public without formal riding clothes. But Grace was the daughter of a multi-millionaire. Grooms did all her dirty work and no doubt she owned rooms full of designer clothes. However, she'd already made it clear she preferred to work with horses from the ground, so breeches seemed overkill.

Maybe Grace wasn't afraid to ride. Maybe she'd just never had much fun with a horse. When Alex had first shown up here, he'd worn crisp white breeches and fitted shirts. It hadn't been long before he switched to blue jeans and T-shirts. And it was her grandfather who'd taught him to appreciate horses and not just see them as a way to win his father's approval.

"Want to sit on Digger?" Cassie asked impulsively. "We can walk down to the brook to cool him out, and I can give you some tips about how to train a horse for swimming."

Grace tugged at her lower lip. "But you'd be holding him?"

"The entire time," Cassie said. "I won't let go of the reins." On a hunch, she added, "And there'll be no one around to see us. The brook is very private."

Grace gave a thoughtful nod, more like an elderly woman than a kid. "Okay, then," she said, turning and hanging her backpack on the hitching post. "I would very much like to accompany you and Digger to the water."

CHAPTER THIRTEEN

Alex slowed his car, waiting as a groom led a dripping horse away from the wash rack. It was almost noon and activity at the barn had slowed. No one was riding in the practice field, or the ring or on the gallop track. The horses that had competed in the polo game yesterday would have enjoyed a massage and mild limbering session, and the remaining fifteen horses had already been galloped. Of course some animals were hurt and simply needed bandaging or hand walking. Like the mare with the bloody ribs. Cassie's horse.

His fingers tightened over the steering wheel. *She was back*. Thank God she'd taken the mare home. He didn't want to hear her voice, or smell her hair or watch her mouth curve in that beautiful smile. Didn't want to deal with the kaleidoscope of memories…along with the painful wrenching of his heart. What they had was in the past. They'd both moved on and he didn't need any reports or updates. In fact, he didn't want to think about her.

She'd been in his mind yesterday though, as if subconsciously he'd been bracing for an encounter. But he hadn't been prepared to see her charge into his barn last night, eyes flashing, fists locked. Prepared to take on

Rachel and her army of staff. Cassie was so damn loyal, so brave. She'd worn that same expression when reporters swarmed the estate, clamoring to interview him after his parents' deadly car crash.

"How does it feel to be sole heir to a fortune?" one particularly unfeeling reporter had asked. "Will you continue with the Sutherland business or kick back and enjoy being a wealthy playboy? Money must soften the blow—"

Cassie had seen the misery on Alex's face and knocked the recorder from the man's hand, threatening to charge them all with trespass. She'd chased them down the drive, insisting that even the servants' entrance be locked. Then she'd sat up with him all night, listening to his bourbon-soaked ramblings while he drank himself into oblivion. She was his trusted friend, his staunch ally, the only person who understood his motivation.

His parents had never been more than squabbling figureheads, too busy pursuing their own activities to notice their only child. But he'd always thought that some day he could earn their approval, if not their attention. When he was older, smarter, wiser. Maybe when he was a better polo player or a more astute investor. But that couldn't happen now. The car accident in Germany had shattered that hope.

Rachel had swooped in the next evening, eager to comfort him and grabbing the role of supportive ex-girlfriend. That's probably when it had happened. He'd always been careful to use a condom during their turbulent relationship, despite her assurances she was on birth control. But somehow she'd wiggled into his bed, clearly entranced with his newfound wealth. He'd been disgusted with both of them, reminding her that their relationship had been over for months.

"We'll see," she'd said, giving a smug smile.

That weekend had changed his life. Not that he regretted it...much. Grace was his responsibility, his life, his joy. And he was determined not to saddle any child of his with the disinterested parenting he'd experienced. Even if it meant being stuck with Rachel and her jealous rages. He might be destined to sleepwalk through life but he could certainly stick around and protect his daughter.

He and Rachel had generally cordial relations. She presided over the house and stable, while he stuck to the poolhouse. Grace never saw them fight. Usually it worked out. But sometimes Rachel crossed the line and he had to put his foot down.

Like now.

He pressed off the ignition and stepped from the car.

"Good morning, Mr. Sutherland," a groom called politely. "Would you like a horse saddled?"

"Not today, thanks," he said. He rarely rode now that Grace had quit riding, and he never lingered around the stables when Rachel was around. "Is Grace inside?" he asked.

"No, I haven't seen her all morning. Rachel and Santiago are still here though."

He glanced around the paddocks, rather puzzled. When he'd left earlier for a meeting, Grace had been with the housekeeper, but he'd assumed she intended to go the stables. Now that school was out, she spent all her time here, playing with the kittens and whatever horse the grooms deemed gentle enough for her to handle.

Her love for animals wasn't surprising. Generations of

Sutherlands had been raised on the estate, and they'd all possessed a deep appreciation of fine horseflesh. It was a little disappointing Grace didn't want to ride with him anymore. He was careful not to push her, but sometimes she looked so wistful when she watched Rachel.

He remembered that look. It was the same one he'd worn when he was a kid, when all he wanted was his parents' attention. He'd been determined to excel at everything, from schoolwork to equestrian events and eventually the family business. But they'd barely noticed. His father had been interested in Alex's riding only as a cover for his extramarital affairs while his mother had been absorbed with luncheons, travel and her Fortune 500 friends.

Naturally, self-centered people were focused on their own gratification. He understood that now. His parents had been happier when they were pursuing their own interests...and not listening to his mundane little problems. His mother had never once asked about the horse show weekends with his father, and he'd learned to keep his mouth zipped. Keep the family intact, protected at all costs.

And now, protect your child.

He strode into the barn, his jaw tight. Keeping Rachel supplied with a barn full of polo ponies made her a more tolerable mother, one less inclined to take out her frustrations on Grace. He and Rachel both knew the operating rules. But yesterday her spitefulness had surfaced. Grace had been upset about Ginger's cuts...and so had Cassie.

He swept into the office without bothering to knock.

Rachel was posed prettily on the sofa, still in her riding

clothes. Santiago lounged in a leather chair, legs propped on the mahogany desk. The man straightened, his boots hitting the floor with a thud.

"Darling," Rachel said, rising gracefully. "We were just talking about the team and how we'd benefit from better practice players. The grooms are okay but not good enough. Perhaps we could bring up some more players from Argentina?"

Alex ignored her hand on his arm and glanced at Santiago. "Give us the room please."

Santiago's eyes met his. Then the man nodded and bolted from the office with a pleasing amount of speed.

Alex waited until the door clicked shut. "The Sutherland polo team will be disbanded," he said, "if I ever see spur marks like I witnessed last night." Rachel gave him an innocent smile. He still marveled at how angelic she could appear. No doubt about it, she was a physically gorgeous woman. But one who left him cold. Fortunately he now knew what was inside that calculating head.

"Perhaps I didn't have my best game yesterday," she said. "But that mare was disobedient and needed to be taught a lesson. Besides, she's an unknown. She'll never step foot on any polo field again."

"Are you pretending your treatment had nothing to do with the owner?"

"Whatever do you mean? Who is the owner?" Rachel batted her long eyelashes and gave a puzzled pout. But that maneuver no longer worked with him.

"You'll notify the Club," he said grimly. "Let them know Jake Edwards' mare is talented and highly trained. And that your poor riding was the real issue."

She jerked in horror and finally there was genuine emotion on her face. "But I can't do that. I'm working toward my plus three rating."

"You'll be working in an empty barn if you don't rectify this," he said.

"You wouldn't do that. We both know Grace would hate a barn without horses. She might be afraid to ride but she enjoys being around them." Rachel's voice turned wheedling. "Besides, it's the one thing my daughter and I share, the only place where we can spend quality time together."

"And where is Grace now?" he asked.

"Maybe with the kittens," Rachel said. "Or out by the paddocks. You know how she loves puttering around with the grooms."

"Who told me Grace hasn't been here all morning."

Rachel gave a careless shrug, completely missing his point. Her hand tightened on his forearm. "Maybe you could play again? With you on the team, we'd be invited to the British Beach Championships. I've always wanted to do that. And this fall—"

He shook off her hand and strode from the office. She hadn't even noticed Grace's absence. Wasn't at all concerned. But that only meant he had to be a better parent to compensate.

He called Grace's cell but there was no answer. And she hadn't responded to his earlier text. The housekeeper confirmed she hadn't seen Grace since breakfast.

He gripped his phone, trying to remember their conversation the night before. After they walked Cassie home, they'd turned on a movie. Neither of them had been very interested. Instead, Grace had peppered him with questions about horses and films and what it was like to jump off a horse's back into a brook.

He'd slipped into his office a few times, once to call his mechanic and arrange for trailer tires and a tow. And the other to call the President of the Polo Club, ostensibly to check on his regular donation, but really to see if Rachel had trashed Jake Edwards' mare. Which she had, of course. He knew his ex-wife all too well.

Perhaps Grace thought he hadn't been listening last night. And maybe he had been a little distracted. Hell, yes, he'd been distracted. He hadn't been able to stop thinking about Cassie, about their walk in the dark, about her infectious laugh...and how incredibly, her left hand was still ringless.

No doubt Grace had noticed his preoccupation. And thought she had two parents who didn't give a damn. She'd been unusually quiet at breakfast too. Not sad though. Nothing like her terrifying episodes last year when she'd stopped eating and psychologists had advised that the best way he could help Grace was to love her mother.

While loving Rachel was impossible, outwardly cordial relations were not. And having both parents reside on the estate had always seemed like the best solution.

He glanced down the L-shaped aisle. Grace had to show up soon. There weren't many places a young girl could go, especially one who didn't ride. She wouldn't leave the kittens alone for long. But the only person in sight was a stocky groom, soothing a gray horse as she applied some ointment to a cut fetlock.

He dragged a hand over his jaw. Then he strode into the tack room and lifted the lid of Grace's tack box. It was crammed full of the usual paraphernalia: brushes, boots, sunblock and the overpowering smell of horse liniment. Her latest riding helmet still had the price tag attached. There were sunglasses and ointments and a variety of colorful bandages.

But the tack box didn't look as full as usual. There was a yawning gap in the middle. Then he realized…her pink backpack was missing. And he had the sinking suspicion he knew exactly where Grace had gone.

CHAPTER FOURTEEN

Alex drove up Jake Edwards' rutted driveway and turned off the car engine. Two horses stared curiously from their paddocks. Nothing else moved.

The house and barn were the same weathered gray, but Jake had invested in a big blue mounting block. It could be for training purposes or maybe the old guy was stiffening up. Otherwise, everything appeared unchanged. Even the wheelbarrows looked the same: dented, oversized and awkward. They'd been much too unwieldy for a little girl to handle, and Alex had pushed a lot of them.

He walked toward the barn, politely calling hello before stepping inside. But the aisle was empty. A horse shuffled in the straw, then stuck her pretty head over the stall door.

"Hey, Ginger," he said, recognizing the mare. He paused to scratch her jaw. She pressed at the door, eager to join the horses outside. She smelled of ointment and wore a purple mesh flysheet with the Sutherland initials monogrammed on the side. Clearly, Grace had been here.

Relief flooded through him, quickly replaced by an odd ambivalence. He didn't want to be here, didn't want to see Cassie. Didn't like to acknowledge that every one of his senses had kicked into a higher gear. Leaving him feeling totally alive.

He turned away from the horse's stall. Grace must have walked across the fields, following the route they'd taken last night. He should have anticipated she'd want to check on the mare. But she couldn't be allowed to visit here again. Rachel had always resented his friendship with Cassie. She'd have a fit if she knew of this visit. And Grace would be the one to suffer.

He remembered Grace's horror when she discovered all her goldfish floating belly up in the aquarium. Rachel had denied unplugging the filter but the fish had died a day after Grace's questions about his favorite instructor...and he'd talked a little too much about Cassie and Jake.

Sighing, he stepped from the barn and walked toward the house.

Three mismatched chairs sat on the porch. He remembered the day Jake had pulled the third wooden chair from the back of his truck. "Cassie saw this at the dump. And thought you needed a place to plant your royal ass."

He'd tried to act cool. It was only an old wooden chair that someone had tossed. But his chest had swelled two sizes that day. He'd been so proud to have his own spot on Jake's porch. A place he belonged. They'd relaxed there at the end of every day, talking about the horses, what training had worked, and what hadn't.

He'd even carved his initials on the back with Jake's pocket knife. And then helped Cassie, who insisted on printing her entire name and had cut her finger in the process. The words were still on her chair: CASSIE EDWARDS. And maybe his initials were still on his chair too.

He yanked his head away and impatiently rapped on

the screen door. He didn't want this shit. Besides, he was a little annoyed. Cassie should have called, told him Grace was here. Or at least sent her home.

And that was so patently unfair, he felt a prick of shame.

"Hey," he called, clicking open the screen door. No one was around. The den and kitchen were empty. Nothing was on the table except the little wooden rooster they had all rubbed for horse show luck. Amazing that they still had it.

His gaze shifted to the left and his breath stalled. Jake was lying on the faded sofa, sprawled on his back. His face was so pale for a moment Alex thought he was dead. And then the man's thin chest lifted and it was clear he was simply sleeping.

Alex pulled in a relieved breath and edged back outside, careful to keep the screen door from clicking too loudly. Dammit, Jake didn't look well. Or maybe it was just odd to see him napping. Still, if he'd suffered a heart attack it was good he was sleeping, taking it easy.

Alex walked back toward the barn. Jake's truck was here but there were four dirty stalls and only three horses. Cassie might be riding the fourth horse in the field but that still didn't explain where Grace was.

Unless she was already walking back home.

He pressed Grace's number, part of him hoping she'd answer and confirm she was on the way back. That way it wouldn't be necessary to see Cassie. However, Grace didn't answer; in fact he heard the distinctive ring tone of her phone. And his mouth lifted in an involuntary smile. Grace was still with Cassie.

He followed the ringing around the barn and spotted

Grace's backpack, hanging on the hitching post beside a well-worn saddle. He put away his phone and checked the saddle pad. It was damp with sweat but drying in the sun. So Cassie had ridden the fourth horse and was presently cooling him out.

She sometimes rode bareback down to the brook. On a hot day, it was a treat for both horse and rider. No doubt, Grace had gone with her, curious about the old swimming hole.

He swerved to the left of the elm tree, easily picking up the trail. Hoof prints cut the ground, marking the path like road signs. It was rough ground though and after all the walking Grace was going to be a very tired girl. No doubt, she'd be happy to climb into his car and drive home. And on the way back, he'd tactfully suggest she not mention this outing to her mother.

One thing for sure, Grace couldn't come back here. Rachel would be furious, and it wasn't worth the hassle.

He needed to find out how long Cassie was staying. Once she returned to California, he'd arrange for a groom to come over and help Jake with his animals. That should ease some of Cassie's concerns. She'd have to smooth it out with her grandfather first though. Jake was a proud man and had scorned all previous offers of help until Alex had just quit trying.

Rachel was still annoyed that he'd assigned the south field to Jake, doubly bitter when he informed her she could no longer ride there. Grace had been a newborn at the time and Rachel had almost dropped her on the cobblestones. She'd seen Alex's incredulity, his utter terror, and realized then that their child was the perfect weapon.

He snapped off a low-hanging branch, automatically

clearing the trail for riders. Yes, it was critical to avoid any more contact with Cassie. He was impervious to Rachel but Grace wasn't. And she idolized her mother. Even though she refused to climb back in the saddle, she lingered around Rachel, trying to help with the horses, desperate to earn the smallest crust of affection.

Just as he'd done with his parents. And seeing Grace's wistful face made him ache.

"I want to see her happier," he'd warned Rachel. "Pay Grace more attention. Or there's no reason for us to continue this charade."

Rachel had dutifully nodded and set aside Tuesday evenings for mother and daughter shopping and Grace's clothes had become a little more chic. And Grace had smiled a bit more.

But it wasn't real emotion, not like Cassie's giggle whenever he'd tickled her or the horrified squeals when he dunked her in the brook or her challenging grin when she galloped fearlessly across the field. And maybe that was the problem. He was always remembering, wishing...

He shook his head, his stride turning more purposeful. He'd hustle Grace out of here, let Cassie know he'd help Jake in any way possible. But Grace couldn't be allowed to return. Besides, Cassie was busy with her grandfather. She didn't have time to entertain a solemn young girl who barely smiled and was terrified of riding.

Laughter bubbled from the brook. And then a telltale splash. He knew that sound—clearly a cannonball. So there were other kids here. He rounded the corner and jerked to a stop, staring in disbelief.

His daughter—who refused to swim in their pristine pool because she thought she was fat—was dripping wet.

Her hair clung to her face and she was laughing uproariously. Best of all, and most unbelievable, she was sitting on a bay horse's back.

"This is the most important thing," Cassie said, her voice bubbly and full of fun. "You want Digger to think this is a good place to come. That standing quietly in the brook brings rewards. Like another handful of grass."

She stepped from the water, stooped and plucked a handful of grass. Alex's throat dried. She'd stripped down to her panties, and when she bent over he could see the delightful curve of her ass, the outline of each rounded cheek, the tapered smoothness of her thighs.

"Remember how he fidgeted when I first rode him into the brook?" Cassie asked, smiling up at Grace and waving the grass.

She must have been underwater too, Alex thought blankly. Cassie's shirt clung to her breasts, and her bra was a lacy white, revealing the pointed outline of her nipples.

He gulped and dragged his gaze back to Grace. She'd swiveled around on the horse's back, both legs hanging on one side, appearing surprisingly relaxed.

"Digger's sure standing good now," Grace said.

"He learned that it's easier to stand in the brook and eat grass, than to neigh and jump around on the bank and have to trot circles," Cassie said. She was back in the water now, the water lapping around her chest, not quite covering the swell of her breasts.

"This is how we train them for the movies," Cassie said. "Very gentle and consistent, just making sure they're rewarded at the proper times. And you helped me train him today, so thank you very much, Grace. You're a natural."

Alex's heart kicked. Cassie loved kids, had frequently taken time at shows to linger and let children pat her horse, often letting them sit in the saddle if she thought it safe enough. He'd warned her she was a lawsuit waiting to happen but she'd just pointed to the kids' delighted smiles and said some risks were worth it. Thank God for that because today Grace was the one benefiting from her generous nature.

His gaze shot to the horse. The animal didn't appear to lack spirit. He looked like a Thoroughbred, probably one Jake had picked up cheap from the track and brought in for retraining. The horse's ears were tilted forward, his attention on Cassie. He wore a bridle but no saddle, and his black mane was soaked. But he looked content to stand in the brook, surrounded by two soaked and grinning girls.

And such longing shot through Alex, it hurt to breathe.

He waited another moment then turned and retreated up the path. No way was he going to intrude. His daughter was in good hands. She was safe, having fun with Cassie. Best of all, Grace was laughing.

CHAPTER FIFTEEN

Water dripped from Cassie's hair, plastering her shirt to her skin. But the wet T-shirt kept her wonderfully cool as she climbed the rough path from the brook. Both she and Grace had pulled off their jeans before taking Digger into the water so at least she wouldn't have to change before riding the next horse.

Grace sat on Digger's back, still smiling and talking non-stop, so relaxed she wasn't even gripping the horse's mane. She sounded much more normal now, like the kid she was, a marked contrast from her earlier formality. Her shirt was as wet as Cassie's, her hair even wetter, and her reserve had been left somewhere back at the bottom of the brook.

"Digger sure is a nice horse." Grace leaned forward and brushed a horsefly off the bay's glistening neck. "Bet my parents would buy him for me."

Cassie made an unintelligible sound. There was no chance Gramps would sell Rachel Sutherland one of his horses, not after yesterday. Besides, Digger wasn't at all suitable for Grace. Sure, he was perfectly behaved when being led, and after a bit of coaxing, he'd stood quietly in the brook and let Grace crawl all over him.

But he was fast, agile and much too responsive to leg

pressure. He wouldn't understand Grace's bouncing seat or her swinging legs. Grace was a beginner and needed a horse with far less spark. Considering her background, it was a mystery why she didn't already own a suitable horse.

"Did you have a pony when you were younger?" Cassie asked, keeping her eyes on the wooded path ahead. She'd already learned that Grace opened up more if she didn't feel like she was being watched.

"Yes," Grace said. "I had Lady and Stillwell and Jazzy, but they all bucked me off. And they were small and stubborn and Mom said they were smarter than me. Polo ponies are different. They're not really ponies anyway. Isn't it weird that a Thoroughbred can be called a pony just because he plays polo?"

"I think that expression started in India," Cassie said. She hesitated, wondering if Grace was deliberately trying to change the subject. The girl seemed to open up about certain subjects, then clamp down on others. And Cassie just wanted her to have a fun morning. "So," she said, "did you ever ride a bigger horse? One the size of Digger?"

"A little bit," Grace said. "But I never liked how I looked when I was riding, you know…"

She paused but Cassie didn't fill the silence. She kept her gaze straight ahead as she led Digger and his rider up the path. Something rustled in the brush and a squirrel scolded from the trees. But it was quiet enough to hear Grace's increasingly agitated breathing.

"Breeches make me look gross," Grace finally said, her words coming in a rush. "Don't tell anyone though. It's embarrassing and then they want me to talk about it with the psychologist. And I'm not going to."

Cassie couldn't help glancing up at Grace's face. So that was the real issue. And the reason Grace was happy to ride Digger. No one was around to see, and today she wore jeans instead of tightly molded breeches.

"It's okay for riders to wear comfortable clothes," Cassie said gently. "You don't always have to dress for a polo match or horse show."

"We do at our stable though," Grace said. "Everyone has to. It looks more professional. And Mom says it makes you a better rider."

Cassie wiped some water drops off her forehead. Alex had believed that too until he took lessons from Gramps and realized that jeans didn't hurt his equitation. "The most important thing," she said slowly, "is to be safe. Wear boots with heels, don't be distracted with your phone and always wear a helmet."

"Not like this one though," Grace said, giggling again. "Your helmet is way too big. My parents would have a fit. They're anal about my safety." She shoved the dented helmet higher on her head, still laughing at its fit.

Cassie tightened her grip on Digger's reins. The helmet was definitely poor protection and she needed a reality check. She liked Grace but she couldn't forget the girl was an heiress. And her parents hadn't given her permission to come here. To ride in a brook with an ill-fitting helmet, on a spirited Thoroughbred. And while Cassie would never shrink from any confrontation over Ginger and Gramps, she'd clearly overstepped with the Sutherland's daughter.

Alex had kindly replaced the trailer tires but he would be as incensed as Rachel if he thought Cassie was influencing his daughter. And rightly so. It was never acceptable to interfere with someone else's child. And he doted on Grace.

"Can we go down to the brook again tomorrow?" Grace asked.

Cassie couldn't control her horrified shiver. What if Grace had been hurt today? "I don't have time," she said. "I need to work with the horses, and I want to spend time with Gramps."

"But I can look after Ginger. And groom and clean stalls too. I could do it in the mornings while you're riding. Then you'd have even more time to see your grandfather."

Cassie's mouth lifted in a reluctant smile. She hadn't had time to clean the stalls yet so having Grace around would be a real benefit. The girl might not have the confidence of her parents but she possessed Alex's desire to help. Still, the idea of a Sutherland child shoveling manure didn't sit right.

"It's summer," Cassie said. "Don't you have friends you'd rather hang out with?"

"I had a friend once but she moved away. Mom used to invite other girls over from my private school but they all rode way better than me."

Cassie froze midstride then forced her legs to keep walking. Grace really was lonely. But she shouldn't be so competitive. "Someone will always ride better than you," Cassie said. "Someone will always ride worse. That's life, just like everything. But you should—"

She pressed her lips together, cutting off the rest of her sentence. She needed to shut up. No 'you should' or any other well-meaning advice. It would be folly to say anything more. Rachel and Alex would resent it, and Gramps was already facing horrible rumors. The Sutherlands could make his life miserable; Rachel already had. More reason to sell his polo ponies quickly and help him leave this insular horse world.

Besides, the little brook ride, though enjoyable, had eaten up several hours of valuable time. She still had all the stalls to clean and two horses left to ride. Gramps would be ready for lunch soon and she needed to contact other polo clubs. Let them know he had four well-trained horses for sale before Rachel had time to smear his name.

"I think," Cassie said slowly, "that you should go home now. Before your parents worry. And I don't have time for any more brook rides. I'll clean the stalls later, when it's cooler."

"I understand," Grace said. "But may I come back tomorrow and help with Ginger? If that's okay?"

Her tentativeness was back and there was also hurt in her voice. For a moment Cassie winced with shared pain. This girl just wanted a friend. Under normal circumstances it would be great to have her hanging around. Cassie loved encouraging kids, and movies that involved young riders were always her favorite jobs. But Rachel would be livid.

And last night Alex had made it clear he also didn't want any association with Cassie. He'd walked her home because he wanted to delete that phone recording. There'd been no mistaking his vehemence when he denied Grace's request to learn about training a horse for swimming.

And today Cassie had done that exact thing.

"You can't walk over here again." Alarm raised her voice. "And I think your parents would prefer you to spend time at your own stable. With their good horses and trainers."

"But they don't have to know. I can sneak across the back fields."

Cassie's wet shirt didn't seem so comforting now. In

fact, she felt bone chilled. Alex had been furious the first time she walked to the Sutherland Estate alone. She'd been seven years old, and it had been a boring summer because she'd fallen and broken her arm and couldn't ride or swim. But she'd found a pretty blue robin's egg on the ground and needed help putting it back in the nest.

Her grandfather hated to be interrupted when he was training horses so she'd hurried across the south field to the Sutherlands', running almost the entire way. Alex had been in the middle of a riding lesson with a coach his father had flown in from England. But he instantly dismounted, passed his reins to a groom and kneeled by her side.

"What's wrong, Cass? How did you get here?"

He'd listened intently, but his face had turned all stony when he learned she'd walked. One of the Sutherland chauffeurs had driven them back in a white limo and Alex had poured her some cold lemonade from a little fridge in the car. The driver had waited while Alex climbed the tree and replaced the robin's egg.

But she could tell he was annoyed. And before he left he walked right out in the middle of the round pen and talked to Gramps. Then Gramps told her she could never cross the fields alone and if she ever wanted help, she was allowed to interrupt him when he was training. After that Gramps was more aware of where she went, and it was all because Alex didn't think young girls should be alone, especially in a lonely field surrounded by country roads.

"You shouldn't walk across the fields alone," Cassie said, her voice firming. "I'll drive you home today, but you better not come back again."

Grace's lower lip trembled and Cassie yanked her head

away, feeling like she'd kicked a puppy. But this situation was impossible. And that section of land had a rough reputation, though undeserved.

Neither of them spoke as they emerged from the wooded trail into the clearing behind the barn. Digger started to prance, excited to be home. From inside the barn, Ginger gave a welcoming nicker. Digger immediately tossed his head and skittered sideways, eager to rejoin his friends.

Cassie tightened her grip on the reins. It would be horrible if Grace fell off now, with Digger only forty feet from the barn. She could even break a bone. Rachel would doubtlessly start a lawsuit. The Sutherlands had the best lawyers, and Gramps would lose his home, his barn, everything he cherished.

"You better get off here," she said, abruptly halting Digger.

"All right," Grace said. She looked a little puzzled but gave Digger's neck a pat then slid from his back. When her feet hit the ground, the oversized helmet dropped over her eyes and halfway down her face.

Cassie almost choked with relief. That helmet had been useless and even her grandfather would have been horrified. But no one had seen, and now all she had to do was drive Grace safely home. She'd drop her off at the staff entrance and pray she wouldn't mention her escapade to either of her parents. They'd never have to know.

Grace pushed back her helmet and looked up. Her face lit up in a beautiful smile. "Hi, Dad," she called.

Cassie stilled, then slowly turned. Alex stood in the doorway of the barn, his face shadowed. The sleeves of his white dress shirt were rolled up and he had a pitchfork in his hand.

"Hello, ladies," he said.

"You should have seen me. I was down at the brook." Grace leaped with excitement, gesturing over her shoulder and spooking Digger with her flailing arms. She quickly regained her composure though her grin remained. "It was so much fun," she added, easing away from Digger's swinging hindquarters. "I rode Digger in the brook and Cassie taught me how to teach a horse to stand, just like she does for the movies. And then I rode him bareback all the way home. And guess what, Digger is for sale, and I think we should buy him."

Cassie gave a silent groan. It sounded like she'd been doing a snake oil sales job, taking advantage of a sweet young girl. It was clear Digger was no proper child's mount. The horse was spinning now, head up and snorting, deciding that whatever had excited Grace was probably dangerous and it was best if they all skedaddled.

Cassie took her time calming him, then looked at Alex's face, expecting to see distaste, if not flat anger. But he merely stepped a little further from the barn, listening intently as Grace talked about her awesome cannonballs and how she'd ridden without a saddle and that she hadn't once fallen off.

And then he looked over Grace's head and grinned. And Cassie's heart slammed against her ribs. He looked so much like the old Alex, and he didn't seem angry at all.

"Digger wasn't like this at the brook," Cassie said. "He just got excited now. I wouldn't have let her ride him if it was dangerous."

"I know," he said. His smile faded as his gaze lowered to her chest, and she realized her shirt was still wet. Worse, his scrutiny filled her with a rush of awareness and she could feel her nipples hardening beneath the thin shirt.

"Excuse me," she said, leading Digger past him, hating this unwanted pull of sexual attraction. At least it was darker in the barn and she wouldn't be at such a disadvantage. And maybe he wouldn't pick up on her churning emotions. Wouldn't realize his intent gaze still inspired hot flashes. She'd stay inside and clean stalls until he left. She was surprised to see him, that's all.

And then she led Digger into his stall and was doubly surprised. Alex must have been here a while. He'd cleaned all the stalls, swept the aisle and even filled the water buckets. His sports jacket still hung over a stall door. It had probably been years since he'd mucked out a stall, and she knew she should be grateful. But now she had nothing left to do. And she just wished he'd load Grace up in his car and leave.

She heard him outside talking to Grace and a moment later he stood in front of Digger's stall.

"Thank you," he said softly. "Grace had a great time with you today."

She slipped off Digger's bridle and replaced it with a halter, pretending she was totally composed. "Great," she said. "She had fun in the water too." Once Grace quit fretting about dirtying her clothes. Cassie couldn't remember ever worrying so much about a little mud. It must be because of the restrictive Sutherland dress code.

"She told me she's ready to start riding again," Alex said. "As long as nobody is around."

"Part of it might be that she prefers riding in jeans," Cassie said. "Instead of breeches. She worries about that."

The stall door clicked and Alex stepped in beside her. "What do you mean?" he asked, clearly shocked but careful to keep his voice low. "She said that?"

He seemed to suck up the oxygen in the stall, making it difficult to breathe. "Yes, but she didn't want to talk about it much," Cassie said, surprised her voice sounded so normal. She turned, preparing to snap the lead rope on Digger's halter.

"Wait." Alex reached out, stilling her hand. "Are you sure? She's never even hinted at that to me."

His gentle touch made her skin tingle, all the way to her toes. And he was so close and smelled so familiar, a heady combination of spice and leather that dominated her senses and made something flutter deep in her belly. If she turned her head, her face would brush his chest. But she'd made that mistake before.

She shrugged, using the movement to press back against Digger's solid shoulder. "Girls often worry about their appearance," she said, "especially when they're growing. Maybe she wasn't comfortable talking about it."

"But she was comfortable with you," he said. "I saw you down there. In the brook. It was amazing, hearing her laugh. And I want that for her, the fun, the camaraderie… What we had."

His tone changed and she made the mistake of looking up at him. For a brief moment his expression was unguarded, almost wistful. Then it shuttered. "Is this horse for sale?" he asked. "Grace really likes him."

"Digger isn't the right horse for her," Cassie said, still absorbing that he'd walked down to the brook and seen her stripped to her underwear. Half naked and frolicking like a kid. Teaching Grace to play like a heathen. Yet he didn't seem to mind. In fact, he sounded approving.

"Gramps has been working with Digger for the last

eight months," she said. "Hoping to sell him as a polo pony. He's almost as good as Ginger. By the way, thanks for looking after our trailer. We'll pay you for the tires, and the tow."

"Don't be foolish," he said. "You know how I feel about you and your grandfather."

His tone was rough but tender at the same time, and it left her unbalanced. She'd always known what he was thinking but not anymore. And it hurt that he hadn't looked her up in all those years. She didn't intend to ask any personal questions. But he was standing so close, the way he always lingered in the barn in case she needed help. She probably wouldn't have another chance to talk to him again.

"How long have you been divorced?" she blurted.

"Six years or so." He stepped aside, pushing the stall door back and making sure it was wide enough so Digger wouldn't hit his hips. "We can talk more inside. Your grandfather invited Grace and I to stay for lunch." His mouth lifted in a rueful smile. "And it's been too long since Jake spoke to me, so you can bet I accepted."

CHAPTER SIXTEEN

Cassie felt like she was in a time warp.

She sat stiffly in her chair while Alex and Gramps bantered about the newest training methods, arguing with a familiarity born from confidence and mutual respect. At one point, Alex left the verandah and strode into the kitchen, unerringly finding the jar of peanut butter that Gramps kept in the third cupboard on the right.

"Have some more, Cass," Alex said, passing her half of a neatly cut sandwich and then sliding the other half on Grace's plate. The ease with which he used her old nickname shouldn't have made her flush, but it did.

"This is good," Grace said, chewing enthusiastically and thankfully drawing everyone's attention. "We almost never have peanut butter at my house."

I bet not, Cassie thought. No Sutherland cook would have been permitted to serve peanut butter and jam sandwiches. That had been the staple here though. Gramps had been too busy to make complicated meals. Besides, next to lobster sandwiches, peanut butter and jam were still her favorite. On her birthday once, Alex had surprised her by adding sliced bananas and that had been good too. He'd always brought great lunches.

"Tomorrow I'll bring the food," Alex said, as if reading her mind.

She gave a nonchalant shrug. But then the full significance of his words hit and she reached for her water glass, surprised her hand was so steady. "So you plan on lunching here again?"

"I want to enroll Grace in daily lessons."

He spoke as if her grandfather ran a formal stable.

"Gramps hasn't given lessons in years," she said. "And sorry but we don't have a suitable lesson horse."

"I can ride Digger!" Grace scrambled from her chair and wrapped her arms around her father's neck. "Thanks, Dad."

They acted as if money could buy everything. And usually the Sutherland money could. Cassie shook her head and looked at her grandfather, anticipating his blunt refusal.

But Gramps just leaned back in his chair and nodded. "Grace wants to have fun with a horse," he said. "I can't help her right now but you're here, Cassie. Seems a shame if you couldn't take the time to teach her a thing or two. Especially since teaching kids is what you enjoy the most."

His reproachful tone made her stiffen. Obviously he and Alex had talked while she was down at the brook, and whatever differences they had were resolved. But her grandfather's defection stung. He and Alex had always seemed to partner up, simply because they shared a masculine view. It had bothered her then, and it bothered her even more now.

Especially since this involved Rachel's daughter. And lessons might be good for Grace but they wouldn't be good for her.

She shot a hard look at Alex. Last night he hadn't wanted to see her again. And if she were honest, that's what hurt. He cared about his daughter's happiness but Cassie was expendable. Always had been.

"Grace," she said, "would you please go inside and fill the water pitcher?"

Grace gave an obliging nod and scooped up the pitcher. Cassie waited until the girl was inside and out of ear shot.

"I'll teach Grace," she said to Alex, "but you'll have to sign a waiver. And I still don't believe Digger is quiet enough. It will only undermine his training and make him harder to sell. So my lessons will be expensive." She quoted an absurdly high price but Alex didn't even blink.

"Also," she pulled in a deep breath. She no longer had proof after Alex had erased her phone recording—and he seemed to trust that she wouldn't be so sneaky that she'd try to record Grace again. However, this last condition was non-negotiable. "I don't want Rachel around Digger," she said, "or anywhere on our property, not after how she treated Ginger."

Alex didn't deny Rachel's cruelty, or even try to defend her. "I'll be the one to drive Grace," he said. "I just want her to have fun. You've always been the best person for that. And I'll find a more suitable horse after you evaluate her riding. You won't have to worry about Digger for long." Then he gave a reassuring smile, his expression surprisingly tender.

Cassie wrapped her hands around her water glass, fighting the urge to press it against her warm forehead. He had no business looking at her like that. It left her hot, edgy and confused. She'd hoped a chauffeur would drive Grace. But a part of her leaped at the thought that Alex would be around.

Of course, his presence would help Gramps. It was

always beneficial to be in the Sutherlands' good graces. And if she rekindled Grace's love of riding, Alex might be so pleased he'd ask Santiago to give Ginger another try. Maybe he'd even tell the Club to remove Ginger from their black list.

She set down her glass with a decisive thump. "All right," she said. "Have Grace here tomorrow at eight." And because it felt good to have power for a change, she couldn't resist adding, "And don't be late. Or you'll have to clean the stalls again."

His chuckle was quick and amused, and so damn attractive she couldn't help but smile back.

Ten minutes later he and Grace drove down the driveway, and she was finally free to hold the glass against her hot forehead and try to steady her breathing.

"It'll be nice having a kid around again," her grandfather said, watching the car disappear beyond the trees. "Alex spent a lot of time here. Makes sense his daughter would like it too."

"I suppose," Cassie said. "I'm surprised you'd want Grace here though. Her mother deliberately hurt Ginger. And she caused a lot of trouble for you."

"But Alex already talked to the president. Jonathon Stiles called this morning and apologized for any misunderstanding. He assured me Ginger wouldn't be on their banned list. Rachel realized she was wearing the wrong spurs for such a well-trained and willing horse."

Cassie jerked forward, almost dropping her glass. "Rachel said that?"

"Apparently almost verbatim. So Ginger is allowed to compete at the Club again. With any rider."

"So the college sale could still happen?"

"Yes." Gramps gave a satisfied nod. "And now that Grace is coming here, Rachel will have to be on her best behavior."

Cassie leaned back in her chair, relieved that Gramps knew what he was doing. She'd been worrying about the polo club, the lies Rachel might be spreading. But the fact that Rachel accepted the blame meant she listened to Alex. Not only had he looked after their trailer, he'd made Rachel call the Club before Cassie even agreed to teach their daughter.

Just because he hadn't said much about Ginger's condition, and had destroyed the phone evidence, hadn't meant he condoned it. She'd forgotten how loyal he was—to his friends, family and animals.

"I don't imagine Rachel liked that much," Gramps went on, his tone gleeful. "Being forced to call the Club and publicly announce she'd ridden poorly."

"No," Cassie said slowly. "I'm sure she didn't like it."

"Nothing she can do though." Gramps chuckled and folded his hands over his lap. "Ginger's here now. All our horses are safe."

Cassie gave a little nod. But she couldn't forget Rachel's cold eyes and how people like Santiago jumped to do her bidding. And she shifted in her chair, jerking forward and then back again, not nearly as comfortable as her grandfather.

CHAPTER SEVENTEEN

The sun beat down on Grace's shiny new helmet, dust rising in spirals as she trotted Digger in the round pen.

"Sit up," Cassie said. "Remember to look where you're going. Digger will move in the direction of your eyes."

Grace glanced to her left and Digger immediately changed direction, so fast she had to grab his mane to stay on.

"Wicked," Grace said, awkwardly repositioning herself in the saddle. "It's cool how he turns on his own. I just wish he didn't do it so fast."

And that was the problem. Digger was too well trained. Not only was Grace perilously close to falling off, it wasn't good for Digger. Her grandfather had worked countless hours to fine-tune the horse to a rider's commands, and Cassie didn't want to dull Digger down. Especially since there was a possibility the college would still consider him for their polo team. Those riders would need a responsive horse.

At least Grace was smiling. She didn't seem in the least bit afraid and Digger was a good-natured horse, the type who tried hard to please his rider. Even if he didn't understand why she kept bouncing around in the saddle.

"May I try riding with a polo mallet tomorrow?" Grace

asked.

"Not yet." Cassie jumped down from her perch on the top rail. "It's best to practice hitting the ball on the ground first. Without horses."

"Okay," Grace said. "Is that how you learned?"

"Yes, and I chased hundreds of balls on foot." In fact, Alex had paid her a dollar for every ball she retrieved. She thought he had a horrible shot, always losing them in the tall grass. It wasn't until later that she realized he'd been trying to slip her some extra cash without offending her grandfather. And both he and Gramps had been adamant about not letting her carry a mallet until they were sure she wouldn't hit her horse's legs. "After I finish the groundwork," Grace said, stopping Digger beside Cassie. "I want to try a belly shot. They look cool."

"No," Cassie said quickly. "Not on my grandfather's horse."

"But Mom does them all the time."

Cassie's mouth tightened. It wasn't surprising Rachel took risky shots. Swinging into a horse's legs required considerable finesse…and a rider needed to be very wealthy to replace all the horses that were lamed up.

"Is that really what you want to do with a horse?" Cassie asked, thinking of the many other riding disciplines Grace might like. "Play polo?"

"Yes." Grace gave an emphatic nod. "Some day I want to be as good as Mom. But I never want to play in front of strangers. And I don't want to ride at home. I prefer quiet places, like here."

Where no one could see her, Cassie thought. Although obviously Grace didn't worry about riding in front of her dad.

Cassie glanced over her shoulder. Alex sat with her grandfather on the porch, within view of the round pen but thankfully not too close. Even from this distance though she was acutely aware of his presence. Could catch the rich timbre of his voice. She'd always loved that voice, how he could keep it level in any situation. She'd only seen him truly upset twice. The first when his parents died and the second when he came to her house to tell her about Rachel...

She turned her back to the verandah. She and Gramps were being paid top dollar for these lessons, and Grace deserved the full deal. Certainly not an instructor who was distracted by a man's voice—the girl's father, no less.

"Are there any other kids who ride at your stable?" Cassie asked. Sometimes the mere presence of boys caused girls to worry about trivial things. She remembered complaining to Alex about not being invited to a classmate's party because the invites only went out to girls with big boobs. The very next day her red-faced grandfather had driven her into town to buy her first bra.

"No other kids," Grace said. "Just Mom and Santiago and the grooms. But they're all old. And I don't like to ride in front of them. So I'm not going to. Ever." Her voice quivered and Digger tossed his head, picking up on her agitation.

"I understand," Cassie said. But she didn't. The Sutherland Estate was a horse lovers' paradise with two riding arenas, a gallop track and a polo field along with miles of private trails. The tack and viewing room resembled a penthouse suite with air conditioning, hot and cold drinks, and fresh fruit delivered daily. Not to mention a beautiful barn filled with top-notch horses. Although it was unlikely any of the Sutherland polo ponies would be a good mount for a beginner.

Grace was comfortable with walk, trot and canter but only if Digger didn't make any sudden moves. And she wanted to swing a mallet but not worry about her horse taking off at an aggressive gallop. She needed a sound, level-minded animal that wouldn't be confused by a rider's mistakes. But one who was trained for polo. And a horse like that was hard to find. People rarely sold them. They placed them with trusted friends or, if they were lucky enough to have the resources, kept them as a cherished member of the family.

"It's really hot," Grace said. "Can we go down to the brook before lunch? I know the way. Maybe I can ride Digger by myself?"

Cassie swiped at her forehead and reached for the lead line. She was hot and hungry and needed to make Gramps lunch, but there was no way Grace could ride Digger alone down that path. "No, I'll lead you," she said. "Digger can move fast. He wouldn't even know he was doing anything wrong."

"But I didn't fall off once today," Grace said. "I thought we were doing great."

"You are," Cassie said. "Both of you. But he's not a child's horse. I think your dad is looking for something more suitable."

It would take a while to find an appropriate horse though, even with Alex's money. Especially since Grace wanted to meander down to the brook, then turn around and hit a ball in an unfenced field. Polo ponies weren't lazy. Or slow. And a swinging mallet would only fire them up. It was like putting a racehorse in a starting gate and expecting them to come out at a sedate trot.

If Gramps were healthier, he could train a horse for Grace. Matching horses with riders had always been his specialty. Or maybe she could do it…

But this was crazy. She gave her head a shake. Rachel employed Santiago, a six-goal handicap player from Argentina. She hadn't hired him only for his looks; the man was truly a wizard on a horse. Surely he could teach a quiet horse to accept a swinging mallet? It sure seemed that Grace was long overdue for a horse of her own.

"Have you ever played polo?" Cassie asked curiously. "With your mom or dad?"

"With Dad, a long time ago when I had a pony. It was fun too. But Mom thought it best if I quit, you know. It was only wasting his time since I can't ever play on a real team."

She spoke so matter-of-factly Cassie could only stare in confusion. There were always youth teams, family teams and mixed teams. Players' handicaps were added together so everyone could compete. Riders were restricted only by time and money, and clearly Grace wouldn't have that problem.

"Why can't you play on a team?"

"I'm left-handed," Grace said. "So Mom and I decided it was best that I stop riding. But we can't tell Dad." Her voice lowered to a conspiratorial whisper. "He gets mad easy, and we don't want him to make Mom move out."

Cassie just gaped in disbelief, then realized she'd stopped breathing. And that she was staring too hard at Grace who, of course, looked away and quit talking.

"I see," Cassie said, looking down and adjusting the lead line. But her mind whirled. When Grace was relaxed, she let out nuggets of information. It was much like peeling an onion, with Rachel the center of a rather stinky core. But was the woman so self centered that she'd manipulate her own daughter?

Part of Cassie wanted to probe. But it was wrong to pump a kid for information. And it still hurt to hear Alex and Rachel linked in the same sentence. She didn't want to feel like this, had told herself she was over him. But she'd probably always love Alex.

Despair rose in a wave. More reason not to get too close to Grace who was obviously just desperate for a friend. It would only end badly. But Cassie couldn't let Grace keep thinking she could never play polo.

"I'm left-handed," Cassie said quietly. "But I learned to swing the mallet in my other hand. And you're younger than when I started so it'll be easier for you to learn."

"You're a leftie like me?" Grace's eyes widened. "But Dad said you're a good player."

"I was okay. And you can be even better if that's what you want."

Grace's eyes remained an incredulous blue. "I don't understand," she said. "Mom told me I could never play." Her gaze shot over Digger's head and she clamped her mouth shut and straightened in the saddle.

"Your grandfather ate his lunch," Alex said, his voice coming behind them. "And went inside for a nap."

Cassie glanced over her shoulder. Alex stood by the rail. Today he'd replaced his dress shirt and tailored pants with jeans and a T-shirt, and it was obvious he'd do anything to encourage Grace to ride again. Even if it meant reaching into the back of his closet.

He probably had no idea Rachel had filled Grace's head

with ridiculous ideas. And Grace said she was afraid her dad would get angry. Yet Alex was the most level person Cassie had ever met. She'd always appreciated his composure, especially since Gramps was so gruff.

"I brought sandwiches," Alex said, holding up a silver thermal bag. "It's hot so I thought we should walk down to the brook and eat."

"You two go," Cassie said. "I'll grab something inside. Just be sure to keep Digger on a lead line."

"Okay," Alex said. "But be careful not to wake your grandfather. He's lying on the sofa. And we did bring your favorite sandwich."

"Peanut butter and banana?"

"No, lobster."

Cassie's head shot up.

"We have pecan squares too," he added, his gaze intent on her face. "I recall you once ate an entire tray of those."

"I don't remember," Cassie said. But she did. The Sutherland cook had been cross and Alex had intervened, claiming he'd been the one who ate them all. She'd never tasted anything as good as those squares. Gramps didn't make desserts and it had been Alex who introduced her to a variety of culinary delights.

"I'll just take out a sandwich and square," she added, eyeing the lunch bag. "And eat in the barn."

"No, sorry," Alex said. "I'm paying for a full day of lessons. So we need a working lunch."

"Actually Grace's lessons stop at one o'clock."

"But it's only noon."

Cassie shoved a tendril of hair off her face, unsure if he was joking. He'd never been a clock watcher but it was true she charged an hourly rate. And eating a peanut butter sandwich alone in the barn wasn't very appealing. "Do you still have the same cook?" she asked, thinking of all the delicious meals she had in the Sutherland kitchen.

"No," he said, "but we have the same recipes. I've learned old favorites are always the best." His eyes locked on her mouth, his expression softening. It was clear now he'd been teasing about quitting early. And also that he stood distractingly close.

He'd rolled up his shirt sleeves yesterday, exposing his muscled forearms, but this T-shirt hid even less. And she resented the flutter in her belly, the way her body sparked just being around him.

Behind her, Grace gave a delighted squeal. "A picnic! That will be so much fun. And we can swim too, if Digger doesn't mind."

Cassie wet her lips. Digger wouldn't mind but she definitely would. Because she remembered what Alex looked like without a shirt, and it was obvious he was even more ripped now. The Sutherland state-of-the art gym was clearly getting a lot of use.

"We can all swim," Alex said. "This is the hottest day so far this summer."

"I'll eat lunch with you," Cassie said, dragging her eyes off his chest and trying to focus on his face. "But I don't have time to swim. I'm not even that hot."

Alex's gaze dropped, skimming over her neck, her chest, and lower. She could feel the telltale itch of perspiration, the way her shirt clung to her navel, and his slow perusal made her even hotter. And now her nipples hardened against her bra in the most annoying way. She wanted to wipe the sweat off her forehead and at the same time cross her arms, but it was more important to remain unfazed. To appear cool and unaffected, just like him. Even though she was burning up.

"Just lunch then," Alex said, his voice gruff. His gaze settled back on her face, and thankfully he was too much of a gentleman to say another word about the heat.

CHAPTER EIGHTEEN

Cassie shifted on the shaded bank, inching further away from the splashing water. She didn't know how much longer Alex and Grace would stay in the brook but one thing for sure, he was a wonderful father. Just like he'd been a wonderful friend.

He held Digger's dripping lead rope while Grace demonstrated yet another cannonball. He didn't seem to care that his clothes were soaked. Fortunately he hadn't taken off his shirt. However, it hadn't escaped the splashes and now clung to the sculpted outline of his back. He was much bigger than she remembered—she'd think him rather imposing if she didn't know him so well—and a little sigh escaped.

Seeing him take such loving care of Grace tugged at her heart, yet at the same time filled her with disquiet. He was the same man she remembered…always looking out for the people he cared about. Unfortunately that no longer included her.

"Remember to jump into the drop-off," he cautioned for the fifth time.

"I know, Dad." Grace rolled her eyes. "Cassie already told me. And she doesn't have to hold Digger. He stands still for her."

"Well, of course." Alex looked over his shoulder and shot Cassie a wink. "But what do you expect? She's a hotshot movie trainer."

Cassie smiled back. He'd always done that, made sure she felt included even when he and Gramps were occupied with other things. And a warmth spread through her chest, somewhat easing the band of hurt.

He hadn't contacted her, not once, but it was clear he was still a friend. It was just that his life centered around Grace now while she clung to old memories. And maybe after having this time together, she could finally move on.

"Let's tie Digger," he was saying to Grace, "and go eat. Before Cass eats all the food."

Cass. The way her heart jumped whenever he used her old nickname proved it might be difficult to move on.

"Okay," Grace said, turning and wading from the water. "I guess Digger is tired." She tugged her jeans back on, struggling to pull them over her wet legs. She didn't appear at all self conscious—definitely not like a girl who was embarrassed to wear tight breeches. "I'm going to pick Digger some grass," Grace added, "so he has something to eat too."

Alex tied Digger to a tree and dropped to the grass beside Cassie. "Last week," he murmured, "she wouldn't even get on a horse. Now she's having fun again and brimming with confidence. Thank you." He reached out and gave Cassie's shoulder a squeeze.

She'd told herself she was content merely to renew their friendship but her rush of awareness was shocking. Her skin tingled, seeming to memorize the imprint of his hand. Even the pit of her stomach tightened and it wasn't from hunger.

He'd already turned away and was unzipping the lunch bag, thankfully unaware of her reaction. "I have some feelers out for a quiet horse," he said. "So far, everything's too hot."

Hot. She stared at his strong, beautifully shaped hands, the blunt curve of his fingernails, the dusting of dark hair on his wrists. She'd seen them do so many things, from soothing her excited horse to wiping away her tears when she fell. They'd tugged her ponytail when she'd been acting stubborn, then patiently taught her how to shift gears so Gramps' truck wouldn't stall. They'd punished a boyfriend when she caught him cheating and later demonstrated the real art of making love. She'd never felt so complete with anyone. Before or since.

She jerked her head away, wishing she could control the flood of memories. Those times were in the past. Clearly he and Rachel had figured out some sort of relationship that worked for them. And more importantly, worked for their daughter. There was no doubt Grace was the focal point of his life. Grace was also the only reason he'd renewed his friendship with Gramps.

And with her.

Now it was time to think like an instructor and concentrate on earning her ridiculously high lesson fees. "Grace needs a quiet all-round horse," she said, reaching down and plucking a blade of grass. "But she wants to play polo too. With all the horses you own, don't you have something that's suitable?"

He shook his head. "We had a few good ponies in the barn but Grace had a couple falls and refused to ride again. Her psychologist didn't want her pressured into riding. Thought the presence of the ponies made her upset."

Cassie rolled the grass between her thumb and forefinger, unable to imagine Alex ever pushing a child to ride. When she was little and Gramps assigned her a particularly nasty horse, Alex had always stepped in, tactfully distracting her grandfather and riding the horse himself. Rachel must have been the aggressive parent. She'd always wanted to be the best. Always needed to top the glamour crowd. Maybe she'd expected too much of Grace.

Cassie knew Alex would never assign blame. He'd always been very private, as well as loyal, never criticizing his parents or allowing anyone else to. The fact that he'd mentioned Grace's psychologist was huge.

"But you'd never push Grace," Cassie said, choosing her words carefully. "You'd never push anyone."

"No. I wouldn't." He slid a plate on her lap. "Let's eat."

She stared down at the lobster sandwiches. Four perfect triangles with the crusts cut off. He'd even placed a pickle on the side. It was clear he didn't intend to talk about Grace, or criticize Rachel. But there had been an odd tone in his voice and there were new lines bracketing his mouth. When he wasn't smiling, he seemed troubled. And she couldn't control her empathy. She wanted to help, wanted to leave knowing he and Grace would be able to enjoy riding together again.

"I'll call my boss when we go back to the house," she said. "Check if he has anything suitable. Some kids in the last movie needed bombproof horses. He won't sell his animals to just anyone, but if you can guarantee a good home..."

She paused, reluctant to bring up a prickly subject, but Rachel's callus treatment of Ginger couldn't be ignored.

She pulled in a fortifying breath, then her words came in a rush. "And you'd have to promise that Rachel would never ride him."

Alex's mouth tightened but he didn't protest or even pretend Rachel hadn't cut Ginger. "She won't be allowed to hurt Grace's horse," he said.

It was clear that was all he intended to say. But it was enough. Because his word had always been rock solid and she still trusted him implicitly. He hadn't said he'd stop Rachel from riding the horse, instead he'd used the word 'hurt.' And that was a little weird, but at least he could control Rachel.

Or thought he could.

◆

"You already shipped the horses back?" Cassie squeezed her phone in disappointment, glad Grace was still in the barn with Digger and wouldn't realize she'd lost out on a movie horse.

Alex shifted his chair on the verandah, sitting so close now his knee brushed her leg. "I can fly a horse back," he whispered. "No problem."

Cassie nodded but knew Alex's money wouldn't make any difference to her boss. If Dan Barrett sent horses back to his Montana ranch, it meant he'd decided to keep them. For future movies or for retirement. And he wasn't the type of man to change his mind.

She spoke to Dan for another few minutes. He even asked some concerned questions about her grandfather, along with the blunter question about when she'd return to work. But by the time they cut the connection she still hadn't found a horse for Grace.

"Dan doesn't have anything suitable, but he'll keep an eye out," she said, placing her phone on the table, using the movement as an excuse to inch her knee away from Alex's leg. Unlike her, he seemed unfazed by the contact. Didn't seem to realize how just the brush of his leg made her pulse race.

"Sounds like you have a good relationship with your boss," Alex said. "That you get along well." He spoke in a statement but there was an undercurrent of interest, hidden in the same careful tone he'd used when he returned from college, asking questions about her latest boyfriend.

Her heart gave a little kick. Maybe Alex wasn't so immune after all. "Yes," she said. "All the directors want Dan Barrett for their horse movies. He's really helpful. Taught me a lot."

Alex crossed his arms. "So Barrett's been around awhile? Worked on a lot of movies?"

"Yes, some big ones. He did *Reckless*, the movie where they discovered a real murder while they filmed. He said he'd never had so many weird things happen on a set."

"I gather he's quite experienced," Alex said. "An older guy?" His expression hadn't changed nor did the texture of his voice. But she knew him too well. Could feel his carefully controlled interest.

"He's about your age," she said. "Crazy that he just trains horses because he's better looking than most movie stars." She gave a vague smile, not about to admit that Dan was happily married to one of her best friends.

Alex lifted his glass and took an abrupt swig of lemonade. The line of his tanned throat rippled when he swallowed. He lowered his glass and she pulled her gaze away, pretending she hadn't been studying his reaction.

"It must be interesting working on movie sets." He spoke slowly, almost reluctantly. "Meeting all those actors. I know about the equine center in West Virginia. But after you left that job I lost touch. Heard rumors you were working in the movie industry but didn't know any details. Your grandfather certainly wasn't talking. How did you end up in California?"

Her composure slipped and now it was her turn to reach for the lemonade. She'd been devastated when she left, still reeling from his decision to marry Rachel. About the only thing she'd retained was her pride and she intended to keep that. So by the time she lowered her glass, she was able to summon a cool smile. "You mean after you dumped me?"

He winced.

"It took awhile to get over you," she continued. "And I was working hard, staying busy with horses. They let me gallop the most rambunctious ones. No one ever wanted to ride them but they were a piece of cake after Gramps' horses. One of them was owned by Dan Barrett. He saw me and offered a job." She shrugged. "I'm not sure why Gramps avoided you all those years. I don't think he ever realized we'd…hooked up."

Calling it a hookup was blatantly wrong for what she had felt for their three-week love affair, but somehow she managed to keep her easy smile. She could feel his scrutiny, the intensity of those intelligent eyes. And then it was impossible to maintain her façade. Her mouth cracked, just a bit, but it was obvious he saw.

"Oh, Cass." He reached out and wrapped her hand in

his. "I never loved Rachel. But no child of mine was going to grow up like I did. I had to try and make it work."

She thought the worst anguish was over but now she was ambushed by fresh pain. She understood his deep sense of responsibility. And in a way admired it. But he hadn't contacted her, even after he was divorced—and that hurt. Now he was holding her hand, speaking so tenderly, and dammit, she could tell he still cared.

And once again, her skin heated from his touch. His thumb moved over the sensitive skin on her wrist, making her pulse jerk along with her heart.

"You and Rachel are divorced," she said, staring at his hand over hers. "Yet you still live together?"

"I stay in the poolhouse. My office is set up there. It's not ideal, but it works."

And Grace had two parents around, just like he always wanted. She tugged her hand away, feeling sad and cold and hopeless. The same emotions she had when he told her Rachel was pregnant. When his eyes had been wet with tears and she'd seen the anguish on his face. And that underscored why she'd been wise to stay away. He was divorced. But nothing had changed.

She pressed her shoulders against the unyielding slats of the chair, wishing she didn't have to see him every day. But Grace needed support and she was in a position to help. Even if, ultimately, it would only improve Grace's relationship with her mother. And therefore with Alex.

"Hopefully I can find Grace a safe horse before I leave," she said, forcing a breezy smile. "So she can have fun riding with you again."

"You've always had a big heart," Alex said. "Thank you, Cass."

He was still leaning forward, one hand resting lightly on his knee, scant inches away. His gaze lowered to her mouth, his eyes darkening. She could sense his interest. If she tilted her head, he'd probably lean in and kiss her. Maybe for old time's sake, maybe for the start of something more.

But he couldn't give her what she wanted. So letting that happen would be a huge mistake.

She rose from the chair, so quickly it scraped back, the grating sound loud on the quiet verandah.

"No problem at all," she said. "That's what friends are for."

CHAPTER NINETEEN

Alex swerved around a gaping rut, too preoccupied to totally avoid hitting the hole. Little wonder Cassie's trailer had ended up with a flat tire. He'd send a private crew to repair the blacktop. It would be quicker than relying on the government. The south side of the county was always the last to be awarded paving projects.

He'd be delighted to buy Jake a new trailer as well as tires, but knew the man would refuse. It had been frustrating watching Cassie struggle as a kid, and he'd insisted on taking lessons from Jake long after he could learn any more from him. Of course, Cassie was just as stubborn as her grandfather about accepting his money. But he didn't like to see the worried look on her face. Never had.

Clearly Jake's place was in rough shape. Fences sagged and a strong wind could blow the roof off the barn. Cassie couldn't stay home more than a few weeks, and it was obvious from the phone call with her boss that the man wanted her back soon. There had to be a way he could help without rousing their prickly independence.

Nine years ago his guilt had prompted him to transfer ownership of the south field to Jake. Cassie wouldn't take his money, and the field was a prime piece of real estate.

Maybe Jake could sell it. However, it adjoined the Sutherland land and it would be a shame if it were sold to a third party. What Jake really needed was an infusion of cash in a way that wouldn't hurt his pride.

The only other things Jake had of value were his four polo ponies. But it wasn't feasible to buy them. Jake and Cassie didn't want Rachel riding their horses. They'd seen how she treated Ginger and didn't trust her with their animals.

Frankly, he didn't trust Rachel either.

Beside him, Grace bounced in the passenger's seat, still talking nonstop about her fun day at Cassie's barn. He gave another distracted nod but his thoughts remained wrapped around Jake and Cassie.

If they managed to sell their horses, Jake would have a cash cushion. But then Cassie would leave. And he liked having her back, even if it was just to teach Grace. Even if that's all it could be...at least for now. His hands tightened around the wheel and he nearly hit another gaping pothole, then realized Grace was asking him a question.

"Lobster sandwiches are almost as good as peanut butter, don't you think?" she said. "I ate nearly as many as Cassie. Would you buy me some faded jeans, just like hers? And I can keep them at her barn."

He glanced sideways. Rachel looked after Grace's wardrobe. In fact, it was unusual for Grace to even talk about clothes, but the hours with Cassie had left her relaxed and chatty. "Sure," he said. "But why keep them at Cassie's barn?"

Grace shifted on the seat and he swung his gaze back to the road. She'd grown into a reserved child, weighing every word before speaking, as if afraid of making a mistake, so this new chattiness was a marked improvement. And something he wanted to encourage.

"Why keep them at Cassie's barn?" he repeated. "In case you get wet in the brook?"

"No," Grace said. "It's just that I don't mind wearing jeans over there." She fiddled with her seatbelt, her hair falling like a wall around her face. "She doesn't care that I'm fat," she whispered.

He whipped over a bump, the low-slung car scraping in protest. Rachel was so obsessed with a perfect image it was affecting Grace. But this was the first time Grace had ever verbalized it. Even the therapists hadn't been able to pull anything out. "What don't you like about the way you look?" he asked.

Grace shrugged then gave her standard reply. "I don't want to talk about it."

Her phone chirped and she grabbed it, clearly relieved to change the subject. "It's Mom," she said, staring at the screen. "I can't wait to tell her about our picnic by the brook. I bet she'd come next time, if you invited her."

He hid his horror with a neutral smile, remaining silent as Grace pressed the phone to her ear and began talking. But the thought of Rachel at Jake's almost made him ill. She poisoned everything. And she'd always been insanely jealous of Cassie, not to mention he'd promised Rachel wouldn't be driving Grace. Plus Cassie was no fool. She knew Rachel wasn't a friend.

"You pay too much attention to that young groom," Rachel had said, the first time he'd brought her home from college. "What are you two always laughing about? And hugging a groom? Really, Alex."

"It's just Cass," he said. "I haven't seen her for months."

Rachel had given that throaty laugh that always reminded him of lush lips and tangled bed sheets. "Darling," she said. "The little groom has to let you hug her if she's on your payroll. But I bet she hates the way you paw her. And it's best to keep staff at arm's length so there are never any misunderstandings." She skimmed a teasing finger over the inside of his thigh, laughing when his cock instantly hardened. "Now forget the barn help," she cooed. "And show me your bedroom."

They'd spent most of that weekend in bed since the day after initial introductions to Rachel his parents had left on an extended European vacation. But he'd refrained from hugging Cassie again, horrified she might think he was a creep. And discomfited to admit how nice it felt when she hugged him back.

He gave a weary sigh. Rachel had always known how to manipulate, even managing to charm his parents. He just hadn't realized until it was too late.

Grace was still on the phone, telling her mother about how Digger and Cassie were so wonderful and how the brook was the very best place in the world to swim. He wished she wouldn't go into so much detail, but he wasn't going to confuse Grace by asking her to keep secrets. She had to deal with enough mind games from her mother. He wasn't going to throw any more at her.

Thankfully by the time he punched in the security code and the wide gates swung open, Grace had put away her phone.

"Stable or house?" he asked, cruising up the smooth driveway.

"Stable," Grace said. "I need to check on the kittens. And Mom wants to talk to you."

Great. He hid his aversion and veered along the pavement toward the barn. White rails gleamed in the sun, and sleek horses nibbled at lush grass. Once this area had been his refuge, the only place his father had ever shown him any attention.

"You're my only son," his father had said, tossing him a riding helmet. "And I expect you to maintain our family fortune, do your duty…and don't ever tattle to your mom. It's a dirty bird who shits in his own nest. Now climb up on that pony and make me proud."

Alex had only been six at the time, but he'd nodded solemnly. Duty meant being responsible, even when it wasn't fun, and not tattling meant never talking about his father's absences. And his dad loved it when he jumped his pony over big fences. "Horsemanship is in his blood," his father would boast to his mother. Pretending they'd been riding together all day even though flowery perfume still lingered on his father's clothes.

And sometimes his dad actually spent a few minutes watching him ride. Equestrian sports were always the easiest way to grab the old man's attention. One time, he and Cass had even held a circus, standing on their horses' backs and doing all sorts of crazy tricks. His dad had been mildly impressed, moving him up to polo lessons immediately afterwards. But Alex hadn't wanted to play polo. It was Cassie who made riding fun. He'd only wanted his father's approval.

Just like Grace wanted Rachel's.

He pulled up by the stable door. Grace was halfway out of the car before he had time to kill the engine.

Rachel stalked from the barn as if she'd been waiting. She gave Grace a cursory kiss on the cheek—something he knew was more for his benefit than Grace's—then waved her inside and continued toward the car.

He lowered the window.

"You should have told me Grace was ready to ride again," Rachel said, her voice accusing. "Santiago can give her proper lessons."

"Maybe later. Right now Grace just wants to have fun."

"At Jake Edwards' dump?" Rachel's perfect nose curled in distaste. "Really, darling. There's no need for our daughter to go slumming. She should learn from qualified instructors."

Alex checked the doorway, waiting until Grace was out of earshot. Generally he and Rachel tried to be civil. But she'd caused trouble for Cassie and Jake, and already his teeth were gritting.

"What Grace needs is some fun," he said. "With no pressure. So I'll be driving her over to Jake's every morning. For as long as Cassie agrees to teach her and as long as they have Digger. And don't make Grace twisted about this. If I see any hint of conflict, hear any whisper that you've given her a hard time, all the polo ponies will be gone. Along with Santiago and every other one of your toys."

"Now you're just being cruel." Rachel blinked in exaggerated horror. Or maybe she wasn't faking. Money and status meant everything to her. She hadn't been able to find that in New York. Thank God the Sutherland lawyers had insisted on a prenup, and she was only living in the house as long as it suited him. And Grace.

"I'm tired of your games, Rachel," he said, wearily pressing the ignition. "And if you continue playing them with Grace, we'll have to discuss other living arrangements."

"You've changed." Her eyes narrowed in accusation. "And I can't leave. We both know Grace wouldn't enjoy spending weekends with me in a cramped apartment." And though she pretended righteous indignation, there was a definite complacency in her voice. They both knew he would never trust a living arrangement where Rachel was alone with Grace. And Rachel would never give him sole custody. It was the perfect stalemate.

On the positive side, Grace had both her parents. She deserved her happiness. And he was determined to give it to her.

CHAPTER TWENTY

"How are Ginger's cuts?" Gramps asked, peering up from the sofa and rubbing his eyes. "Think you'll be able to put a saddle on her soon?"

"Another couple days maybe," Cassie said, as she wrapped up the extra lobster sandwiches and stuck them in the fridge. There weren't many dishes to wash since Alex had kindly brought Gramps lunch as well. Not a lobster sandwich but a huge chicken casserole from the Sutherland kitchen. A relief really, because she had trouble finding food Gramps liked, and she feared he wasn't eating enough calories.

"Grace is giving her great care," Cassie added. "She made a special ointment and brought a flysheet so we can turn her out. And Grace really likes Digger. She spent a lot of time picking grass by the brook, feeding him before she ate her own lunch."

"She's a nice kid," Gramps said. "Glad she's having fun. But she's not experienced enough to ride Digger alone."

"No," Cassie said. "She needs a quieter horse."

"Even if she could handle Digger," Gramps said, his face creasing in a scowl, "I wouldn't want Alex to buy him. After what happened to Ginger, I don't want any of my horses near that Rachel woman."

Cassie made an agreeable sound deep in her throat. She didn't want to encourage this topic. Her grandfather was settled on the sofa and she wanted him to remain mellow. But the bloody marks on Ginger were disturbing.

The more she looked at them, the more she questioned that they were even spur marks. They were a little too high, a little too wide. She didn't like to consider the alternative, that they'd been deliberately inflicted. Maybe Santiago had given Rachel some elaborate Argentinean spurs. Either way, Ginger was now out of their reach. And even though Gramps needed the money, it was reassuring that he remained fussy about his buyers.

His eyes were closed again so she tiptoed over and covered him with a light blanket. His color was a lot better today, his face not so drawn. Having Alex around seemed to be a comfort. And it wasn't just because Alex had used his clout to remove Ginger from the black list.

He'd always been helpful, not only with chores but the two men respected each other. And Alex stood up to Gramps in ways she never would. In fact, she was surprised Gramps had ordered Alex to stay away. She'd assumed the rift had been Alex's decision.

Hooves sounded outside, the pounding shattering the serenity. She hurried to the window. Digger was excited, cantering around the paddock with his tail high. And now the other three horses were all spinning circles and copying his behavior.

Digger jerked to a stop, jammed his head over the top rail and stared down the driveway. She followed the direction of his pricked ears, wondering who was coming. Gramps didn't get many visitors, and Alex and Grace had left almost an hour ago.

Moments later a late-model silver truck pulling a matching trailer eased up their narrow driveway. The imposing Sutherland crest was visible on the sides. She shot a confused look at her grandfather. But he appeared to be sleeping, his breathing slow and relaxed.

She eased the screen door open and walked toward the truck.

The driver lowered the window and gave an apologetic smile. "I'm a little early," he said. "But I dropped off a horse at the polo club and it was quicker to come directly here."

"Come directly for what?" she asked.

"A pickup. Isn't this Jake Edwards' place?"

"Yes, but there must be a mix-up. We don't have any horses leaving."

"I'll wait." He tugged at his ball cap, averting his gaze. "I'm only ten minutes early."

Cassie tilted her head, eyeing him warily. Alex had already agreed Digger wasn't a suitable horse for Grace. And he knew she didn't want any of Gramps' horses going to the Sutherland barn. In fact, when Alex watched Grace doctoring Ginger's cuts he'd displayed obvious regret, and also a hint of anger. He'd never said a word about Rachel though…just as he'd never complained about his parents.

"Are you sure you have the address right?" she asked the driver. "What exactly did Alex say?"

"Oh, he didn't send me. It was Rachel."

Cassie squeezed her eyes shut, then crossed her arms and stepped back. "You might as well leave. We don't have any horses for her."

"If you don't mind," the driver said, tugging the visor of his cap even lower. "I'd like to stay. She'll be annoyed if the trailer isn't here when she arrives."

Cassie gave an understanding nod. When she'd worked for the Sutherlands, Rachel had been known to fly into a rage when Alex wasn't around to witness it. And now that she was entrenched as queen of the estate she wielded even more power.

The driver checked his side view mirror. "She's coming now," he said. "Maybe you can straighten it out. Good luck," he added.

Cassie gave the man a grim nod and strode toward the cream Bentley.

Rachel stepped out, still dressed in her riding clothes. Her hair was loose though, rippling like gold over her shoulders, her mouth a bold fuchsia red. Clearly she'd taken time to refresh her makeup though it wasn't necessary. Nobody could deny her beauty.

"I see my driver already arrived," Rachel said. "I'm surprised our trailer fit up your little driveway." She glanced around in contempt. "Doesn't matter. I heard about the horse Grace rode today and I'm here to buy him."

"Digger isn't suitable for a beginner," Cassie said.

"My daughter isn't a beginner," Rachel snapped. "And she can take lessons from Santiago. He's definitely more qualified than someone like you."

"But Digger is trained for polo." Cassie spoke slowly, determined to keep her temper in check. "He needs an experienced rider. He's not safe—"

"You people are just typical horse traders." Rachel gave a dismissive sniff. "Always trying to drive the price up. But I don't have time to bargain. I'll pay fifty thousand, right now."

Cassie gulped. That was the amount Gramps had hoped to receive for their top horse, Ginger. But Digger wasn't as talented and Gramps thought they'd be lucky to get thirty. And that was before Rachel had tried to smear Gramps' name and all his horses.

"A few days ago you said my grandfather couldn't train horses," Cassie said slowly. "I don't understand. Now you want to buy one?"

Rachel shook her head as if Cassie were dense. She reached into her car and pulled out a sleek check book. "No," she said. "I want to buy all four. Fifty thousand each."

Cassie's breath stalled. *Two hundred thousand.* That was more than she could save for Gramps in twenty years. More than enough to set him up for a comfortable retirement. And he wouldn't have to lift a finger. He'd have no more animals to feed, to ride, to worry about.

Of course, he would worry. As long as Rachel was riding his horses, he'd be sick with worry.

Rachel's hand posed over her check, a gold pen between her fingers. "Jake Edwards, is it?" Her voice dripped with disdain. "I don't suppose a place like this even has a stable name."

The woman had a lot of gall. Driving in here and insulting Gramps' home, his business, and not even acknowledging Ginger's injuries. "Our mare is still healing from her cuts," Cassie said. "From the ones you left. And by the way, they don't exactly look like spur marks."

Rachel's head jerked up. For a moment those blue eyes held a trace of fear. Then it was quickly replaced by contempt. "Don't be stupid. Take the money. And then you can leave. Just go back to where you came from."

"We would never let you near Ginger again," Cassie said, crossing her arms. "Not after what you did. I'm beginning to think you cut her deliberately, perhaps before you even mounted. What did you use, some sort of knife?"

Rachel gave a taunting smile. "You can't prove anything. And you're just looking for an excuse to stay. Trying to wheedle back into Alex's life. Well, it won't work. He'll never give up Grace. And he'd never put her in front of a judge."

Blood pounded through Cassie's head, drowning out the sound of Rachel's voice. Her hands clenched so tightly her nails dug into her skin. She'd tossed the knife comment out, more from anger than anything else. But Rachel had just admitted that she'd deliberately cut a horse.

"Don't look so shocked." Rachel's mocking voice seemed to come from a distance. "I took Alex from you before, and I certainly intend to keep him from you now. And there's no need to pretend to worry about my daughter. I'd never jeopardize her on an animal that's too spirited. Santiago will put a special bit on that Digger horse. Teach him to listen. Now, I'll have my man lower the ramp—"

"My horses aren't for sale!" Gramps' gruff voice boomed behind them. "Not to the likes of you. And you need to get off my property. Now!"

Cassie turned. Gramps seemed to have swelled, looking more like the intimidating man who'd swept into the hospital and scooped her into his arms, all those years ago.

Rachel's eyes narrowed. She didn't appear particularly intimidated. She just stared at Gramps, then at Cassie.

"You're both fools," she said. "And you'll regret this." The tips of her perfectly manicured fingers ripped the check in two. Pieces of paper fluttered in the breeze then dropped to the ground.

Rachel gestured to the driver and slid back into her car. She didn't look at them again, or at the horses she'd come to buy. She rolled down the driveway, leaving dust clouds rising in her wake.

Cassie bent down and picked up the pieces of littered paper. "When I first saw her," she said, "I was sixteen. I thought she was so beautiful."

"Yeah," Gramps said. His shoulders slumped and he looked small again. "I had a horse like that once. Damn good-looking. People overlook a lot of faults when something is easy on the eye. But that horse was mean to the bone. Took me awhile to accept."

"How can Alex deal with that?"

"I don't know," her grandfather said. "Marry in haste, repent at leisure. I think Alex is still repenting."

CHAPTER TWENTY-ONE

"Keep the mallet in your right hand," Cassie said, tossing another ball on the ground. "And this time try tapping it through the goal posts. Remember there's no top to the goal. The ball can go as high in the air as you want."

Grace walked up to the ball, her expression determined. She swung her mallet and whack! The ball soared through the center of the goal posts.

It was a beautiful shot. Stomping around the field, hitting and retrieving the ball, was tiring but the ground work definitely helped. Grace had good eye-hand coordination, and now her shot had some power. Her passes were improving too. At least on foot. Those skills had yet to translate to the back of a horse and that would be more difficult, especially since Grace didn't have a quiet horse to ride.

Cassie noted the spot where the ball had dropped by the trees and gave Grace an encouraging thumbs-up. "See, you can learn to play with your right hand. I'll give you some strengthening exercises that can help too."

Grace flashed a triumphant smile. Today she wore shorts and seemed relaxed about showing her bare legs. "This is a great field," Grace said, heading in the direction of the ball. "The grass is cut the perfect length. Maybe tomorrow we can try passing the ball back and forth on horses?"

"Maybe," Cassie said, striding beside Grace. But she shuddered to think of a rookie rider on one of Gramps' high-powered polo ponies, loose in this big field. Grace would have difficulty keeping control, even with two hands on the reins. And when she had one hand holding a mallet, any ride would likely end in a runaway.

"Horses are tempted by open spaces," Cassie said, trying to be tactful. "And Thoroughbreds are bred to run. So we should wait until we find a more suitable horse. I had a lot of falls in this field. Some of them really hurt."

She didn't want that to happen to Grace. It might shatter the girl's newfound confidence. And Rachel's fury would be unimaginable.

"Did my dad fall off too?" Grace asked.

"Sure. But not as much as me. My horses didn't always stop or turn."

"But Dad's did?"

"He was a better rider," Cassie said. "And a lot of times my job was just to canter around the field hunting for his balls."

But because of his constant practicing, she'd been able to raise enough money to buy a real polo saddle. Alex had always been generous. Smart too. He'd known exactly how to circumvent her grandfather's pride. It seemed whenever she needed extra money, Alex had tack that needed cleaning or horses that required exercise.

She'd been forty-five dollars short of buying her prom dress when he suddenly announced he needed his Porsche washed and vacuumed. "Rachel likes a clean car,' he'd said, loud enough so Gramps would overhear. "And I don't trust anyone but you with the paint, Cass."

"I wish we had more than three balls," Grace muttered. "And these plastic ones are all dented."

Cassie blinked and pulled her attention back to the sunny field. She had to stop living in the past. Besides, thinking about all the nice things Alex had done left her softened, vulnerable. She couldn't afford that.

"Mom has buckets of balls in the tack room," Grace went on. "More than she ever needs. I'll bring some tomorrow. It would save us a lot of walking."

"Better not," Cassie said.

"But I think it's okay." Grace tugged at her lower lip. "Santiago won't mind. And Mom won't even notice."

Cassie shot her an appraising glance. Grace said her mom wouldn't notice—not that she wouldn't mind. So Grace either knew or guessed that Rachel wouldn't be happy about sharing Sutherland polo balls. Even if they were for Grace's lessons.

Grace's voice always turned dutiful when she spoke about her mother, as if she were weighing each word. Alex had been that way too, refusing to say anything bad about his parents, even when they forgot his birthday.

Cassie blew out a little sigh. If Alex's parents had been more caring, he might not have married Rachel. Might not be so determined to keep Grace's family intact. Try as she might, Cassie couldn't help but like Grace. The girl was sweet and genuine, and when she dropped her reserve, she was excellent company.

Cassie hadn't been sure Grace would even show up for her lesson this morning, not after Rachel's visit yesterday. But a stretch limo had rolled up the driveway promptly at eight. No doubt Alex was trying to ease Rachel's jealousy by sending Grace with a chauffeur...or else Grace had pressured him to buy Digger and he was annoyed they hadn't been allowed to purchase the horse.

And that was okay too. She'd lived without Alex's friendship for almost a decade. She didn't need it now. And she certainly didn't expect him to accompany Grace every morning.

But somehow the day didn't seem as much fun. She was hot and tired, and it would take awhile to find the third ball. They were often hard to spot in the taller grass behind the goalposts.

"It's almost lunchtime," she said, lifting the hair off the back of her neck so the breeze could cool her skin. "You'd better call your driver. We'll look for that last ball tomorrow. Besides, if you hit much longer, you'll have a sore shoulder."

Grace gave her arm an experimental flex. "It's fine," she said. "And Dad's picking me up after his meeting. So I have time to give Ginger and Digger some grass."

So Alex was still coming. He wasn't *that* worried about pleasing Rachel. Cassie, swept by a surge of relief, let her hair fall back down. Obviously he didn't mind that Gramps had rejected Rachel's offer. Maybe Alex didn't even know about it. Maybe the idea had been cooked up between Grace and her mother.

"You understand why we can't sell you Digger, right?" Cassie asked. "Both he and Ginger are a little too much horse for you. And so are Storm and Tex."

"Oh, yes, I know. Dad said I have to be patient."

"I wondered if you told your mother you wanted Digger," Cassie said slowly. "That you asked her to buy him?"

"No, I just told her I was having lessons in the round pen and that we led him down to the brook. And that you made sure I always wore a helmet and never let go of Digger. I didn't want her to think this wasn't a good place, you know..."

Cassie rubbed her forehead. She'd assumed Grace had asked her mother for Digger. It didn't make sense that Rachel would try to buy a potentially dangerous horse. Yet she'd tried to buy all four of Gramps' polo ponies. Had made a wildly generous offer without even riding them, or having a vet check.

Perhaps she'd just wanted to eliminate any reason for Grace to visit. Which meant her primary concern wasn't her daughter's happiness. It was Alex. Still, that didn't sit right. What kind of mother would endanger her daughter just to keep her ex-husband away from an old friend?

Rachel had showed up only an hour after Grace left, with an empty horse trailer and her limitless checkbook. Bristling with posture and purpose. And she'd been furious when she drove away. Furious but controlled.

That type of anger didn't settle in a day.

"It's really nice of you to offer," Cassie said, "but please don't bring any balls from your barn. We're fine with what we have. Besides, it's good to practice air swings with your right hand. We can end the lesson by swinging at weeds. That's always fun."

She scooped up the spare mallet, determined to distract Grace from the inconvenience of having a limited number of balls. "Let's see who can be the first to knock off twenty dandelions," she said, grinning in challenge. "On the count of three!"

♦

Alex parked in front of Digger's paddock and stepped from his car, instantly feeling his tension ease. At home, dread wormed through him every time he neared the stable. Here, the air was serene. Even the horses looked happier.

Digger jammed his head over the top rail, hoping for a treat. Alex paused to pat the horse. Grace's helmet dangled from a post beside her backpack so obviously she'd finished her riding lesson. They wouldn't have gone to the brook without Digger so they must be in the south field. Grace had mentioned she and Cassie planned to practice hitting balls on foot.

He shook his head gratefully, scarcely able to believe Grace wanted to ride again. She was ready to have fun on a horse, even eager to learn polo. And it was all because of Cassie. She made everything fun.

When his father first dumped him off here, supposedly for riding lessons, he'd wished his old man would have found a more upscale place. But Jake's had been convenient, a world removed from his parents' peers, out of sight yet close to his father's favorite prostitutes. Alex had spent longer and longer hours here, his 'lessons' extending into mealtimes and then into weekends.

The first night his dad didn't bother to pick him up Alex had been close to tears just wanting to go home, even if it meant being alone in the big house. Jake had tossed a blanket and pillow on the sofa, then shuffled off to bed, oblivious to his misery. But Cassie had tiptoed over, her eyes solemn.

"This is Tonto," she whispered, placing a stuffed pony on his chest. "He's my best friend and you can borrow him tonight."

The pony was worn out, one of its glass eyes was missing, and stuffing bulged from a blackened rip in its stomach. But she gave it a reverent pat before slipping back down the narrow hall to her room. He knew she'd lost her parents only eleven months ago. He didn't see his mother and father much but at least they were alive. Yet here she was, giving up her most prized possession.

He was way too big to need a stuffed toy. Besides, he had lots of real horses. He didn't need a fake one. But the pony was soft and floppy and rather comforting, and the next thing he knew it was morning, and Tonto was clutched against his chest.

And now Grace was benefiting from Cassie's generosity, the Edwards' spirit of inclusivity. And Rachel would just have to accept it.

He reached into the back of his car and pulled out a thermal lunch cooler along with a bucket of balls. Polo balls were expensive and easily lost, and Jake had never owned more than a couple. The least Alex could do was make it easier for Cassie to teach.

The front porch was empty so he strode past the little house and followed the wooded trail down to the south field. The path was overgrown and needed trimming, but he knew the way. Feminine voices bubbled from beyond the trees and his stride quickened. He recognized Cassie's laugh but not the second one. He knew it must be Grace but didn't recognize the sound. Probably because he didn't hear it nearly enough.

He stepped out from the trees, his gratitude swelling. Cassie may have been reluctant to teach Grace but they got along well. They were both laughing, heads bent over the grass as they pounded in divots with their boots. Someone had been hitting the ball, and quite vigorously.

Cassie was the first to sense his presence. She swung around, her eyes locking with his. Her hair was long and loose, framing her sweet face, and her mouth lifted in a beautiful smile. A hungry heat filled him and he ached to scoop her up and relearn the shape of her mouth. To hold her close and never let her go. To hell with worrying about Rachel's volatile temper…or the fact that he had nothing to offer.

"Dad!" Grace called. "I can hit the ball now. Really far. We lost the last ball in the grass though so we had to stop."

He dragged his eyes off Cassie's mouth and set the bucket on the grass. "That's great. I brought some more balls so you don't run out. Want to show me your swing?"

Cassie glanced down at the bucket, her smile fading. "That's a lot of balls," she said. "And you're already paying too much for Grace's lessons."

"Those balls are seconds," he said quickly.

"Dented and last year's colors?" she asked, and now there was a hint of mischief in her voice.

"That's right." He chuckled, remembering the line he'd used on her grandfather whenever Cassie needed more practice balls.

"Okay then. Thanks," she said. "We'll try not to lose them."

She gave a grateful smile and his chest flooded with a warmth he hadn't experienced in years. She always made him feel like that: appreciated, alive, happy.

Grace had already grabbed the bucket and dumped out a stream of balls. "Watch this, Dad." She took up a stance in front of the goalposts, clearly confident in her ability. She looked like such a normal kid and Cassie looked so proud. And he couldn't stop smiling. At Cassie, at Grace then back at Cassie again.

"She's doing great," Cassie murmured. "She wants to try hitting the ball from a horse tomorrow. A scare now wouldn't be good though. And Digger is used to chasing balls at speed."

He couldn't stop staring at Cassie, re-absorbing her face, the little dimple in her left cheek, the way a smile teased her lips when she spoke. She used to have a tiny scar at the top of her forehead, courtesy of one of her grandfather's crazy horses, and he felt a flare of panic when he couldn't find it.

Then the wind lifted a tendril of her hair and there it was, precisely where it was supposed to be. He remembered his horror when he saw the blood streaming from her head and thought he'd lost her. He couldn't let her leave again. And though she would never admit it, he could tell she wasn't happy in California. And then her lips weren't moving anymore and he realized she was waiting for him to speak.

"Grace definitely isn't ready to ride Digger with a mallet," he said, his voice gruff.

"Then why try to buy him?" Cassie asked, her dimple no longer in sight. "Rachel came by yesterday. She wanted to buy him, all four horses actually. And I thought we agreed Digger isn't right—"

"Hang on." He blinked in shock. "Rachel? She came here?"

"Yes, with a trailer. You didn't know?"

"No. But we don't talk much." He set the lunch bag on the grass, hating to think of Rachel anywhere near Cassie.

"I'll make sure she doesn't come by again," he said, and

he was swept with such a well of protectiveness he reached out and wrapped his arm around her. And then his other arm rose and he impulsively tugged her into his chest. He just needed to hold her close, just for a few seconds. Just wished he could turn back time.

He squeezed his eyes shut, inhaling her scent, her sweetness, wanting her with every fiber of his being.

"I'm so sorry, Cass," he whispered, and they both knew he was talking about more than Rachel's visit. His hand brushed the tips of her silky hair and he had the overpowering urge to tilt her head and find her mouth.

He glanced over her head, checking that Grace wasn't watching, but already Cassie pushed at his chest. He dropped his arms and let her twist away, and they both pretended absorption with Grace hitting the ball. And he couldn't think of a single damn thing to say.

"I brought lunch," he said.

"No, thanks. I'll grab a sandwich from the house. You're a better shot than me anyway. You can give Grace some pointers."

"But I'm paying you."

"Don't do that," she said. "Please."

"All right." He gave a casual shrug, but hated his sense of panic. She was in total control here. Just her simple 'please' was enough to turn him to jelly. It always had been.

He'd cut an important meeting short, bullied some business partners into submission, just for the chance to sit on the grass and hear her laugh. And he didn't want her toiling in an airless kitchen, worrying about preparing meals for her grandfather after she'd worked so hard teaching his daughter. All he'd ever wanted was to look after her, to be a part of her life, and those old feelings had returned in full force.

He scooped up the lunch cooler, pretending to stagger from its weight.

"Tons of good food here," he said. "Some freshly baked bread your grandfather would like…when he wakes up from his nap. Also some smoked salmon, chocolate éclairs and even some white wine."

She tilted her head, and he could see her weighing the uphill walk back to the house along with the knowledge that she'd have to tiptoe around the kitchen so as not to wake her sleeping grandfather.

"Those are some of my favorites," she admitted.

"Indeed," he said, quickly opening the cooler. "What a coincidence."

♦

Cassie stretched out beneath the shade of an oak tree, eyes closed, drowsy from the food and wine. The smoked salmon was a delicious surprise and this spot had always been the perfect place to steal a nap. Far from the endless chores that accompanied the privilege of horse ownership.

The chirping of birds mingled with the muted sound of Alex's and Grace's voices and the occasional crack of a ball against a mallet. Everything felt normal, and so right.

Like Gramps, she also felt more secure when Alex was around. She let herself drift away, content that for now everything in her world was perfect.

A persistent fly tickled her cheek. She reached up, vainly trying to brush it away. And heard Alex's low laugh.

Groaning, she opened her eyes. "You always were a tease. Never letting me sneak naps down here."

He grinned, dropped the blade of grass and stretched out beside her, so close his arm brushed her shoulder. She knew she should keep more space between them but she was too content, too sleepy...too happy. She'd probably eaten too much for lunch. She definitely had enjoyed her share of wine.

"Grace wants to hit some more balls," he said. "And you looked too peaceful lying here alone."

"She might have a sore arm if she keeps practicing," Cassie warned.

"I showed her a few other drills. But she's reluctant to follow my advice. Doesn't seem to think I'm qualified enough."

Cassie laughed. Alex was a much better player than she'd ever been. Polo players were graded on an international scale, and he was a four-goal handicap, as opposed to her minus one. Even a professional like Santiago was only ranked two goals higher than Alex. And she didn't want to ask questions, didn't like her growing interest in his life, but the words spilled out anyway. "Why in the world did you stop playing?" she asked.

"It was no fun without you."

She twisted, guessing he was joking. But he wasn't smiling. His chiseled face looked more thoughtful than anything.

"And I despised the Club's elitist direction," he added. "It's become very exclusive."

"Maybe you'll play again." She flattened her head back against the grass and closed her eyes. "Now that Grace is interested. You, Rachel and Grace can even play in the family tournament." She waited, hoping to hear him say he'd never want anything to do with Rachel.

"I have to find Grace a horse first," he said.

She was glad her eyes were closed. Relieved he wouldn't see her disappointment. Because against all reason, she'd dared to hope. Obviously there was a good explanation why he'd never called. He simply didn't care enough.

"I had a message from my boss," she said, her voice completely level. "He has a gelding that might be suitable. Was used for some polo scenes last year and knows the game. He was also a stand-in on a couple movies and short films. Might be a good horse for Grace…and Santiago could teach her."

"Horses actually have stand-ins?" Alex's chuckle was quick and amused, and he totally ignored her comment about Santiago.

"Four horses played Reckless in the racing movie," she said. "Dan said this gelding is adaptable so they kept him around thinking they could use him on another polo movie. But he doesn't have enough speed."

"Grace would be ecstatic to have a horse that was in a movie," Alex said. "Do you think he's quiet enough?"

"He worked on movie sets so he's used to commotion. But if he's trained to rear or do other stunts, he could be dangerous."

"Can we look at him? Where's the horse now?"

"At the Three Brooks Equine Center in West Virginia. Too far. I can't leave Gramps that long." She gave a little shrug. She'd love to visit her old workplace and the horse might be perfect, but it was over a thousand miles away. And while she wanted to help Grace and Alex, her grandfather took precedence.

"No problem," Alex said. "We can take my plane."

He spoke about taking his plane like most people talked about taking their car. But his parents had always owned a private jet. Naturally he had one too. "Sometimes I forget how wealthy you are," she admitted.

"One of the many things I love about you, Cass."

His voice sounded odd and she tilted her head, checking his expression. His face was mere inches away and he was looking at her so tenderly it made her breath stall. His gaze dropped to her mouth and the color of his eyes changed, darkening. The air crackled. Even the birds silenced as if alarmed by his intensity.

She couldn't breathe, couldn't think. Could only feel.

His masculine scent surrounded her, leaving every inch of her skin tingling. Her tender nipples jutted against her shirt. Her brain screamed warnings but her traitorous body arched toward him. Even her lips felt thick, full, parting in invitation…

"Dad!"

Cassie jerked back.

"Dad," Grace repeated. She rushed toward them, waving her mallet in one hand, the bucket of balls in the other. "I found every ball I hit. Some of them were hard to see because of those white flowers."

Cassie sat up, her arms clutching her knees. Alex had already risen, his movements unusually stiff for such an athletic man.

"Good job," he said. "And tomorrow Santiago can give you some pointers."

"But what about my lessons here? I want Cassie."

"Everyone wants her," Alex said. His voice shifted as he glanced over his shoulder, his heated eyes locked on Cassie. "But she's flying to West Virginia with me tomorrow. We need to look after some long-overdue …business affairs."

CHAPTER TWENTY-TWO

Cassie leaned closer to the curved window, peering down at the fields as the plane gained altitude. Thoroughbred farms had a distinctive appearance from the air with their white fences and oval training tracks. She hoped the pilot would circle to the east, over the vast Sutherland Estate. Then maybe she could pick out Gramps' tiny farm. However, in seconds a wall of clouds blocked her view.

"Coffee? Fruit?" Alex asked, unclipping his seatbelt. "There are also fresh bagels and muffins."

She gave an appreciative nod, rose and followed him down the plane's short aisle. Her grandfather had still been sleeping when Alex picked her up, and she'd barely had time to grain and hay the horses. There certainly had been no time for breakfast.

"This is a beautiful plane." She glanced around, absorbing the white leather sofa, the surprisingly wide aisle and the spacious food and drink galley. She'd been on chartered flights for her wrangler's job and had flown into some remote locations, but Alex's jet reached a different level of luxury. "Do you use it a lot?"

"Definitely." He opened a gleaming stainless steel fridge and pulled out a tray of pre-cut fruit. "I do a lot of business up here. A plane saves time and is the one place where privacy is guaranteed."

His property was gated so she suspected he was talking about getting away from Rachel. Clearly his ex-wife took a keen interest in his activities. Maybe this was where Alex brought his girlfriends. It was obvious he didn't want any permanent entanglements; his life was devoted to Grace.

But he must be getting sex somewhere. She knew for a fact he was extremely virile. Although maybe he continued to sleep with Rachel. That would explain why Rachel still lived on the estate. And why she was so obsessed about keeping other women away.

Cassie spotted a bed tucked behind a privacy curtain and jerked her gaze away. She didn't want to think about Alex's ex-wife or how many other women he might have. And if he did use that back room to check out the talents of his female associates, it was none of her business.

"A plane makes travel easier," Alex said, his perceptive eyes on her face. "Less time in airports plus a flexible schedule lets me come home every evening. Sometimes Grace flies with me. That bed was added for her," he added. "It's not a casting couch."

"I didn't think that." She fumbled with a bagel. "Not really."

"Yes, you did," he said quietly. "Maybe you've been in the movie industry too long. Have you ever thought about training and teaching back here?"

"Gramps would like that."

"So would I," he said. He passed her a plate. "Do you still like mango? There's some here. Kiwi as well."

She took the serving spoon he pressed into her fingers, barely listening as he teased about how dubious she'd been the first time she'd tasted mango. But her mind was whirling. *He wants me to move back!* That was the first time he'd actually said it. And he certainly wasn't the type to say things he didn't mean.

Her chest swelled with an airy hope and she felt light enough to fly. Didn't need this beautiful plane. She scooped some fruit on her plate, picked up some cream cheese for her bagel and even remembered to add a splash of milk to her coffee. But she was on auto pilot now, her mind whirling.

They'd always been good together, enjoying the same things and making each other feel whole. Already it seemed like they'd never been apart. Alex even looked younger, and the lines around his mouth had smoothed.

He'd seated himself beside her on the sofa, his arm brushing against her while he ate. And it felt so right.

"We don't have much time," he said, almost apologetically. "The plane will be landing in twenty minutes so we need to eat fast."

She was too happy to have much of an appetite so that wasn't an issue. She nibbled at her fruit then took another sip of coffee. She needed to put his words away for now and focus on the real reason they were flying to South Virginia—to find Grace a horse. It needed to be a quick trip. She didn't want Gramps doing any barn chores.

"The equine center is a half hour from the Three Brooks airport," she said. "And the airport is small. So it would save time if we call ahead and book a taxi."

"We're landing at a private strip," he said. "A driver will be waiting on the tarmac."

She nodded, not really surprised that he had already made arrangements or that they were using a private strip. But even Derek Burke, owner of the Center, relied on public planes. When she was young, she'd been accustomed to Alex's wealth—the expensive horses and fancy cars—but now he had even bigger toys.

"You've done well with Sutherland Holdings," she said. "Managing all those investments. I gather you didn't tank its net worth."

"Doubled it," he said.

She almost spilled her coffee. Then she gave his fingers an impulsive squeeze. "That's wonderful." Her voice rang with pride. "Remember those reporters saying a playboy like you would fritter it all away? That the only thing you knew was polo. I wish your father could see what you've done."

"So do I. Maybe he would have been happy about it but I don't know. I've changed some strategies. Our management team is investing more in the Pacific Rim now, not so much in Europe."

"He would have been very proud," she said.

Alex looked skeptical, his expression reminding her of all the times he'd tried to please his parents, only to be disappointed. They'd been so aloof, letting him grow up thinking he was undeserving, barely noticing his considerable accomplishments. Certainly never acknowledging them.

"You were always so good at sports, at school, everything," she said, remembering how he'd tutored her in math when Gramps had thrown up his hands in despair. "I think they were always proud of you. They just weren't very good at showing it."

His spontaneous chuckle made her grin, and they both smiled at each other, because the thought of Alex's parents showing any kind of approval was frankly quite ludicrous. He reached up and cupped her face. "Damn, I missed you, Cass."

His thumb skimmed her cheek, then caressed the top of her lip, his eyes holding hers. Her breath leaked out. She didn't want to tell him to stop, even if she were capable of speech—which she wasn't. Merely breathing was hard enough. Her entire body quivered with desire, his very closeness filling her with anticipation.

Then his mouth replaced the pad of his thumb and her lips automatically parted. Pleasure shot through her as his tongue linked with hers and he kissed her with a hungry intensity. By the time he lifted his head, she clutched his shoulders with both hands, her breath reduced to gasps. A warning sounded on the intercom above her head, and she heard his regretful groan.

"We're landing in ten minutes," he said, his mouth pressed against the side of her neck. And it was obvious that his breathing was every bit as ragged as hers. "We need to move back to our seats and belt in."

He rose and scooped up the dishes, putting everything away with his usual economy of motion. Yet somehow he managed to keep his hand splayed around her hip.

And then she was back sitting in her seat by the window and he was clipping her belt, and his long arm was draped around her shoulders.

"Tell me more about the Center," he said. "And the horse we're going to see."

His hand played with her hair, sending tingles of awareness skimming down her neck. "He's a bay gelding," she managed, trying to turn her thoughts to horses. "Eight years old, fourteen two hands high. Apparently very even minded."

Alex linked his other hand through hers. "And what about the Center? How did you like it? Were you okay when you first arrived?"

When she first arrived. After he'd dumped her for a pregnant Rachel. And then she realized why he was holding her hand, why his arm remained wrapped around her. He was monitoring her reaction.

She knew she'd stiffened but he continued stroking her hair, and she didn't really want to move. Besides, it was easier to be honest, to talk freely when she was pressed against him like this. And he knew it. She could feel his concern, along with the heightened pounding of his heart, and it no longer seemed important to guard her pride. To hide the depth of her anguish.

"I was devastated," she admitted.

She felt the warmth of his mouth against her hair, the press of his lips. "I was too, Cass."

She left her head resting against his chest, her fingers entwined in his hand. "It was probably good for me to leave though," she said. "And make my own way. I might have stayed working with Gramps my whole life."

"So they treated you well? At the Center?"

"The first month was tough. All the best positions went to locals, and I was limited to mucking out stalls and galloping headstrong horses that nobody else wanted to ride. But I worked my way into a full-time riding job. I even galloped a Derby winner once." She couldn't keep the note of pride from her voice. The equine center was an elite spa that catered to racehorses and the company was extremely selective about their exercise riders. She'd been the only one who had never been licensed at a racetrack.

"I can't wait to see the place again," she said, feeling a change in the engines as the plane began its descent. "The staff is probably the same. They don't have much turnover." No doubt she'd still be working there if Dan Barrett hadn't noticed her galloping on the oval.

"And I hope the horse is nice," she added, "and will suit Grace. So this plane trip isn't a big waste."

"This trip is definitely not a waste," Alex said.

His mouth brushed her lips. The kiss, though quick and light, was full of such promise it left her charged with hope. And the knowledge that they had a full day ahead, a rare day to enjoy together, away from Rachel, Gramps and even Grace.

CHAPTER TWENTY-THREE

The entrance to the Three Brooks Equine Center was just as impressive as Cassie remembered, the elaborate cobblestones and landscaping reassuringly unchanged. She'd been numb with homesickness and heartache when she first arrived. But the people and animals had been welcoming and it was an unexpected gift to be able to come back and renew old acquaintances.

A stocky receptionist sat behind the desk in the lobby, her head bent over what Cassie guessed was a crossword puzzle.

"Hi, Frances," she called.

Frances looked up, her jaw dropping. "You're back? I thought you were in Hollywood, acting or something." She thrust aside her pen with a clatter, rushed around the gleaming oak desk and gave Cassie a clumsy but exuberant hug.

"Not acting," Cassie said. "Working with horses. We're here to look at a gelding that Dan Barrett dropped off. This is Alex." She gestured behind her.

"Hello," Frances mumbled. She scooted back behind the safety of her desk. "I'll call Wally for you," she said, fumbling with the phone.

Cassie glanced over her shoulder. Frances had always

been intimidated by attractive and powerful men. Alex was definitely both, even though Cassie had deliberately refrained from mentioned his last name. But his power was ingrained, cultivated from birth. It showed in the way he looked and talked, even the way he moved. Cassie was used to it. She was also accustomed to his perception.

He remained several feet back, as if sensing the woman's discomfort and content with Cassie taking the lead.

"He's gorgeous," Frances whispered, slanting her gaze toward Alex. "Is he a movie star?"

"No. Just a dad looking for a quiet horse for his daughter. Dan Barrett has a gelding here that he can't use. He thought Alex might like him."

Frances visibly relaxed. "Must be a horse in Peanut's barn. All the animals in the Center are racehorses booked for therapy." She paused to speak on the phone then replaced the receiver. "Wally's at the vet clinic but he'll be back soon. Said Dan's horse is in the stall next to Peanut and to make yourself at home."

Cassie gave an appreciative nod, welcoming the chance to wander around and give Alex a quick tour. The Center offered the most advanced equine therapy and had a range of rehab, including an oxygen chamber, vibration plates and a swimming pool. Most of the clients were blue-blooded Thoroughbreds, and it was gratifying how well they performed after leaving the spa.

But she sensed Alex was eager to see the horse first.

"We can go to Peanut's barn now," she said. "And check out the horse. The little barn is on the other side of the parking lot."

"Great," he said. "Is Peanut their flagstone stallion?"

"No." She smiled at the thought. "He's an old pony who belongs to the owners. I don't know his exact age but he's a testament to the health benefits here. He gets regular oxygen and infrared treatment, and has complete run of the property. He's totally spoiled but a darling. Jenna and Emily owned him since they were kids. He's part of their family."

Alex's brow raised. "The Center has more than one owner?"

"Actually Jenna's husband, Burke, owns the Center and her sister, Emily, works in the movie industry with me. She's married to Dan Barrett." She paused, remembering that only a few days ago she'd deliberately let Alex think Dan was single. But she was feeling much more confident now. Impossible not to, considering the way he'd kissed her.

Her eyes lingered on his mouth, causing her belly to give a little quiver. "Dan Barrett is the reason I ended up working in the film industry," she said. "One of the Thoroughbreds was a known renegade and he saw me galloping him. But that horse was child's play compared to riding some of the animals Gramps had in for training."

Alex winced at the memory so she changed the subject, talking instead about how most of the Thoroughbreds had been perfectly behaved, and how she'd loved conditioning them for their return to the track. He was interested in all the available therapies too, listening intently as she spoke about the great results here.

"I was just fortunate the Center was hiring," she added. "Otherwise I would have had to stay home. And it would have been horrible being around you and Rachel." Her voice trailed off and she realized she was revealing far more than she'd intended.

But he just nodded, his mouth tight. "I agree," he said. "It would have been hell having you close. Wanting to see you, knowing we couldn't."

His fingers splayed around her waist and she realized he'd been finding excuses to touch her since they stepped off the plane. It was as if he'd left his responsibilities back in Virginia, along with his reserve. He was so open now, like the man she'd known, even saying he wanted her to stay. She rose on the tips of her toes and impulsively kissed his cheek.

His arms banded around her. "Let's check out this horse quickly," he said, his voice gruff. "Then hurry back to the plane. Tomorrow we can fly somewhere else and look at another horse. And another and another."

She laughed but his mouth was against her neck and it didn't feel like he was joking. "Or maybe we can just grab that little pony," he said. "And squeeze him on the plane. That would keep Grace happy for a while."

"Even you don't have enough money to buy Peanut," Cassie said, fighting the temptation to hurry back to the privacy of the plane. After all, they had the entire day. And horse buying should never be rushed.

She grabbed his hand and tugged him toward the outlying barn. A woman stood in the doorway, watching them with prim disapproval.

"Hello," Cassie called. "We're here to look at Dan Barrett's bay gelding. Wally is meeting us."

The lady's name was Judith and her face visibly softened when she realized Wally had authorized their visit.

"The horse is back here," Judith said. "We call him Freckles. I'm not sure of his registered name or his breeding, but he's a lovely horse to be around. I have a sheet somewhere that lists his commands. He's been in quite a few movies."

Cassie gave a subdued nod. Dan thought the horse might be suitable but Grace would never be able to handle an animal trained to rear or bite, no matter how quiet. It was much too dangerous. Even a pawing horse could mistakenly hit a handler's leg. And it was irresistible for a kid to want to show off a horse's tricks.

Judith jabbed her thumb at a box stall on the right. "That's Freckles," she said. "I'll just check the office for his file."

She strode down the aisle, her steps crisp with purpose.

"A trick horse is probably too dangerous," Alex said, picking up on Cassie's reservations. "Guess we'll have more time on the plane. We won't even have to ride him." He didn't sound entirely disappointed that their horse-buying trip was a bust, and he was already glancing toward the exit.

Straw shuffled and a horse poked his head over the top of the stall door, curious about the voices in the aisle. It was easy to see why he was called Freckles. Blotches of brown speckled a blazed face. His eyes were soft and intelligent, and he eyed them respectfully, not shoving at their hands but clearly pleased to have visitors.

"He's rather cute." Alex stepped closer to the stall, his voice almost grudging. "Well mannered too."

Cassie reached out and scratched the horse's neck. Apparently he was too placid a ride for any polo film. And his spots made him too distinctive for background work. It would be a pain to constantly dye them. But the fact that her boss had kept him around proved he was a nice animal. Dan Barrett knew a good horse when he saw one.

"I found his file," Judith announced, striding back down the aisle and reading from a green folder. "Eight-year-old quarterhorse cross. Ground ties. Suitable for crowds, explosions and water scenes. Vet shots up to date." She glanced up and shrugged. "That's about it. Oh, and his big trick is to bow on command."

Relief swept Cassie. No rearing, biting or pawing. Just a horse who would bow when asked. What kid wouldn't like that? And she'd wanted to find a special horse for Grace. Maybe this was the one.

Alex winked at Cassie, the only sign that he was equally intrigued. He looked back at Judith. "I'd like to ride this horse, please," he said.

♦

Cassie watched as Alex cantered Freckles in a perfect figure eight, the lead changes precise, clean and balanced. He was a superb rider and made every horse he rode look better. Of course he'd taken lessons at a very young age, from a variety of instructors. And he'd excelled at every discipline. His father had made sure of that.

She glanced back at Wally who was staring at Alex in awe. "Damn," he said. "I didn't know Freckles could do that. Guess Dan should raise his price."

But his words were accompanied with a good-natured grin. Wally, like Dan, was a horse lover and more concerned about finding Freckles a good home. She'd always be grateful that he'd hired her, especially since she had no experience galloping racehorses.

"It was nice to see everyone today," she said. "Including Peanut."

"Yeah, that little guy is still a nuisance." Wally gestured over his shoulder at the pony. "Look at him. Acts like he's king of the hill."

Peanut swished his thick tail and sauntered across the manicured lawn, pausing to snatch a bite beside the KEEP OFF THE GRASS sign. His ears pricked when he spotted Freckles. He broke into a bouncy trot and hurried toward the riding ring. The four-foot fence didn't slow him. He simply bent to his knees and scooted beneath the lower rail, emerging at a trot on the other side.

"Wow, he's agile," Cassie said. "Sure doesn't move like a senior."

"Yeah, he's had some setbacks but the oxygen chamber helps. He'll probably be around for another decade, crawling under fences and teasing clients' horses." Wally shook his head but Cassie knew he adored the pony every bit as much as Peanut's owners.

Freckles had stopped cantering and stood in the center of the ring on a loose rein, with Alex tall in the saddle. Both man and horse eyed the loose pony with a similar degree of bemusement.

Peanut seemed to consider Freckles an interloper and charged toward him, ears back and shaking his head. But Freckles ignored the pony's bluster, waiting to take his direction from Alex. Peanut circled Freckles twice then nipped at the horse's hind leg. Freckles simply swished his tail, looking as amused as Alex.

Cassie gave a relieved smile. "Freckles is a confident horse. Nice to see he's unfazed by other animals. That's helpful in polo."

"He's not fazed by anything," Wally said. "We don't have a mallet here but I've stood on his back and swung a broom, brushing cobwebs off the rafters. He didn't mind at all. He'd be great for a nine-year-old."

Cassie jerked her head sideways, surprised he knew Grace's age. Alex was close-mouthed about everything, but especially family. She'd introduced him to Wally but the two men hadn't had much time to talk. Alex had been too busy with Freckles.

"Did Alex mention his daughter?" she asked curiously.

"Must have." Wally turned and jabbed his thumb at the gate. "Alex can ride Freckles along that path if he wants to check the horse out on the trail."

Cassie nodded. She wanted to spend some of this precious day alone with Alex but they'd come a long way and it was more important to make sure Freckles was suitable. It would be horrible to ship him home and have Grace fall in love, only to find out Freckles needed a more experienced rider. Not only would Grace be devastated but Rachel would be…

Cassie squeezed the railing, not quite sure of Rachel's reaction. Only that the woman was unpredictable. And would Freckles even be shipped to the Sutherland stable? Rachel had abused Ginger but that mare belonged to Gramps. Freckles would be okay.

Besides, he'd belong to Grace. Rachel wouldn't hurt her daughter's horse no matter if the animal was remotely connected to Cassie. But as her eyes settled on the good-natured horse standing in the ring, she couldn't control the shivers traveling like spiders down the back of her neck.

♦

Three hours later, she and Alex were in the back seat of the limo, returning to the airstrip, smiling and congratulating each other on finding the perfect horse for Grace.

"This calls for champagne," Alex said. He wrapped his arm around Cassie's shoulders, still grinning. "Thank you, sweetheart. Wally has already arranged for shipping. Freckles will be at your barn by tomorrow afternoon."

"My barn?"

"Your grandfather's. I want Grace to continue lessons with you. At this point, she doesn't want to ride anywhere else. Santiago already reported that she refused to ride with him today."

Cassie gave a quick nod, picturing Grace on Freckles, the girl's laughter as she hit balls in the field and then splashed through the cooling brook. Freckles had proven to be totally bombproof on a trail, and he and Grace would have a lot of fun together. But then the happy images were replaced by Rachel's glittering eyes. And how the woman had tried to buy all Gramps' horses—just to keep Alex away.

She pressed back against the seat. "Do you think that's wise?" she asked. "Having Freckles at my place? What will Rachel think?"

Alex kept his arm around her shoulders, outwardly relaxed. But she could feel the cording of his muscles. He was silent for so long she thought he intended to shrug it off, or else change the subject.

"Rachel pretends to care about Grace," he said slowly. "Acts like she wants her around. But it's only a sham, cultivated so she'd win in a custody battle."

Cassie stilled, surprised he was revealing so much. For Alex, talking about family had always been taboo. Unless one belonged to that family.

"All she wants is the estate," Alex went on, his voice almost rusty. "And what comes with it...riding on the polo team, money, family status. I try to watch her, stop her from abusing her position. But I'm tired of it. All I really care about is Grace." He tilted Cassie's head and stared into her eyes. "And you."

She hadn't realized she'd been holding herself rigid, barely breathing. But this was wonderful. He still loved her. As she did him. And she'd never have to leave him or Gramps again.

He still stared into her upturned face, studying her expression. She felt her lips quivering with a joy so intense it was almost unfamiliar. And then his mouth slanted over hers. But this kiss wasn't like the one on the plane. It was deeper, hotter, hungrier as if the walls had been knocked down and he was intent on making up for lost time.

His tongue entwined with hers and he wedged her tighter against his lap. His desire was obvious and the feel of his familiar body left her aching with need. She slid her hand beneath his shirt, wanting to get closer. Needing to touch his skin, absorb his scent, feeling like she was throbbing and melting at the same time.

He abruptly lifted his head.

She looked around, taking a few extra seconds to realize the car had stopped. The driver remained silent in the front seat, totally professional behind the privacy shield. But they'd definitely arrived at the airstrip. Men in orange coveralls bustled between hangers, and a man in a dark suit stared curiously at the car.

She clutched at Alex's shoulders, surprised she hadn't realized the car had stopped. And just wished the drive was longer. Her lips felt thick and sultry, her entire body tingling. She pulled in a breath, glad the windows were tinted and she had time to regain her composure.

Alex cradled her head against his chest as if understanding she wasn't quite ready to get out of the car. She could feel the beating of his heart, the raggedness of his breathing. And it was obvious he was just as disappointed.

"It's only two o'clock," he said, his hand caressing her hair. "I'm going to arrange for one of my grooms to feed your horses. Drop off some supper for your grandfather. And change our flight plan. Okay?"

Change the flight plan? And then she realized what he was asking. They were going to fly around while they made love. She gave a little choke of disbelief. "That's impractical," she said. "Won't that use a lot of fuel?"

"A whole lot," he said, his voice low and full of promise.

He pushed open the door then turned and held out his hand in invitation. His expression looked like it had that day long ago when he had said that he'd always loved her. When it seemed nothing could stop them from ending up together. But someone had stopped them. *Rachel.*

She shoved that thought aside, reached out for his hand and let him tug her from the car.

CHAPTER TWENTY-FOUR

The plane leveled in the air. Alex rose and very purposefully shut the door between the cabin and the cockpit. Cassie's mouth turned dry, and she was hit with an unexpected twinge of nervousness.

He was the same man she'd slept with nine years ago. But he looked bigger in the narrow confines of the plane. Obviously he'd filled out. His shoulders were broader, his mouth harder, the bulge between his thighs much thicker.

It wasn't the act of making love that caused reservations. They'd shared passionate sex before. In fact, she'd never realized how good it could be until Alex had shown her. But their physical intimacy had ended in a world of hurt. Of course, Rachel couldn't get pregnant again...could she?

Alex shook his head and Cassie realized she'd asked the question out loud. "I haven't touched her in years," he said.

He bent down and unclipped her seatbelt, his blue eyes glittering. She expected him to lead her directly to the bed—his arousal was obvious. But he seated her on the leather sofa and pulled out a glistening bottle of champagne.

"To our new horse," he said.

She picked up her wine glass. He hadn't called it Grace's new horse. He'd said "our." The three of them. And that was significant; he always knew how to reassure her.

He stretched his arm over her shoulders and began talking about Freckles and movie horses and asking questions about how she would train a horse to bow. Talking as if they had all the time in the world. And soon he had tugged her on his lap, his mouth and hands mapping her body, and she stopped thinking about how much he'd hurt her.

He unbuttoned the front of her shirt and fondled her breasts, leaving her shivering with pleasure. "You're sure the co-pilot won't walk back here?" she asked, arching against him even as she took another worried look at the cockpit door.

"I gave strict instructions," he whispered against her lips, his voice smoky. He opened the clasp of her bra, caressing her nipple between his thumb and forefinger. His head dipped, skimming the bottom of her jaw, the column of her neck, the sensitive skin of her inner arm, and the leisurely exploration shot heat directly to her core. His mouth fanned her breast, then finally sucked her nipple, making her sigh.

He gave equal attention to her other breast, his mouth gentle but firm, his touch slow yet masterful. She didn't remember him being quite so attentive and then he was too slow and she arched against him, wiggling with impatience.

He rose and led her to the bed. Yanked back the privacy curtain. His boots hit the floor with two emphatic thuds, his belt buckle clinking as he stepped from his jeans. He had a scar above his hip that she didn't remember and the hair that led to his massive erection looked darker, thicker—

He leaned over her, his eyes raking her body, possessive yet vulnerable with longing. He pulled off her clothes and tossed her panties aside. His hips covered hers, warming her skin with his heat, and she instinctively arched to meet him. Wrapped her legs around him and quit thinking. This was Alex and she knew him. Trusted him. And they joined together like longtime lovers, his hard thrusts filling her with a growing need, driving home just how much she loved him.

He rocked against her, burying himself even deeper and her eyes closed as the convulsions swept her. She opened them for one last boneless quiver, holding his gaze in that moment of intimacy. He gave several last powerful thrusts, his sounds of satisfaction mingling with hers. Then he rolled on his side, pulling her into his damp chest.

"I love you, Cass," he said, his breath ragged. "Always have, always will."

Joy swept her but she was too weak, too boneless to answer. She could only press an affirming kiss against his chest. It was as if they were simply picking up where they'd left off. He was so loyal, so true, and she was back at his side.

She'd call her boss tomorrow, let him know she wouldn't be returning. And she couldn't wait to tell Gramps. Maybe they could train horses together again, just like before. Even teach some children. The local pony club usually needed volunteers and many members couldn't afford their own horses. She'd been so fortunate to have animals to ride, and people to teach her. Now she'd have a chance to pay it forward. And what a great way for Grace to meet new friends.

Alex adjusted a pillow beneath her head, fluffing it up so it had the perfect vee. "I'll have to get a bigger plane," he said, tugging her closer.

"Why?" She loved the feel of his arms, the way he held her against his chest like he never intended to let go.

"One with a higher cruising speed," he said. "Your next shoot is in California, right? We need something bigger. Definitely a bedroom with a door." He chuckled then reached out and adjusted the privacy curtain.

She didn't smile. Her face felt frozen, still pressed against his chest. Frozen and confused. He must be assuming she didn't want to give up her job.

"I was thinking of quitting," she said slowly. "Finding something to do around here. Back home, close to Gramps. There are lots of children who would love a chance to ride, especially on the south side where there are no affordable stables."

She couldn't see his expression but the tightening of his arms revealed plenty.

"That's not a good idea," he said. "Not right now. There's no need to change your life."

Something clamped around her chest and the air in the small cabin felt thick, almost claustrophobic. Her heart was beating double time, leaving a thundering in her ears. But she could hear the throb of the engines, the low croon of music—and Alex's measured voice as he spoke about how it was important to do what was best for his daughter. How he needed to consider Grace.

"When she's eighteen," he was saying, "she'll be off in college. Safe from Rachel."

"That's nine more years."

"Yes," he said. And there was genuine regret in his voice but it didn't make her feel any better. For a moment, she was too stunned to say anything else. But really, it was just like before. Except that instead of the barn, he intended to use a luxury jet as their meeting place. His own mile high club.

She caught her humiliated sob before it climbed her throat, too proud to let it escape. Her hands gripped the sheet and she pulled it over her breasts.

"And perhaps in time Grace will see Rachel's true colors," he added. "So we won't have to wait as long."

"No." Her voice was so flat she barely recognized it. "Rachel's too smart. Too manipulative. She'll make it so Grace always wants to please her."

Alex leaned over, as if alarmed by her tone. "We'll figure it out," he said. "But Rachel will make life miserable for Grace if we're not discreet."

Rachel and Grace. It was always about them. She wanted this so badly she'd deluded herself into thinking it could work, when really all she'd ever be was an afterthought.

"Please give me a little privacy," she said, clutching at the sheet. "I want to get dressed."

"We can stay in the air a few more hours, plenty of time—"

She shot him a glare. He opened his mouth then closed it. His face shuttered and he rose from the bed. She waited until he gathered his clothes and stepped on the other side of the curtain before allowing a single tear to trickle from the corner of her eye. She swiped it away, afraid if the tears started they'd never stop.

All she wanted now was to be alone, far from this humming plane with its cramped toilet and limited privacy. And far away from the man she loved, but the one who seemed forever destined to hurt her.

CHAPTER TWENTY-FIVE

"Looks like Grace's horse has arrived," Gramps said, gesturing out the kitchen window. "You better call Alex."

Cassie closed the training book she was reading and moved to the window. A large horse transport inched into the yard, the driver being careful not to jostle its equine occupant.

"Can you call Alex for me?" she asked, tugging on her boots. "I have to get outside. And maybe it's best if they don't come until tomorrow. That will give Freckles time to settle before Grace shows up."

Gramps shook his head in reproach. "But it's her horse. She'll want to be here."

Cassie gripped the door knob. Gramps was right. Of course Grace would want to be here. But she didn't want Alex around. They hadn't said much after the plane landed last night, and she thought she'd done a good job of hiding her misery. But she hadn't slept a wink, and her eyes were so puffy this morning even her grandfather had noticed.

"Grace doesn't know we went to look at a horse yesterday," Cassie said. "So she might not know her dad bought him. Maybe Alex wants to wait until the weekend or something…"

"He dotes on his daughter. I'm sure he can't wait either. This is a special time for all of us. Just a second." Her grandfather yanked open a drawer and rummaged through the contents, clearly stoked about the idea of anyone getting a new horse.

"Remember this?" he asked, pulling out a blue ribbon with a triumphant flourish. "You kids found it. We can tie it around her horse's neck. I did that for some clients and they always loved it."

Cassie shrugged and pushed open the door. Of course, she remembered that ribbon. But she had to stop trying to make Alex and Grace happy. In fact, she wished Grace would quit coming for lessons. Life would be simpler. Last night, when her tears had been soaking into the pillow, she'd resolved to ask Alex to stay away. She loved him but she couldn't sneak around for nine years.

But now in the daylight, faced with the horrible prospect of never seeing him again, things didn't seem so black and white. Maybe his plane proposal was workable. Surely they wouldn't have to spend all their time in the air? Especially if she didn't return to California.

She could live with Gramps and help him train the tougher horses. And maybe she could teach other children along with Grace. And whenever Alex had time he'd join them and they could all ride together…but only if Rachel didn't know about it. Because then she'd take out her frustrations on Grace and that's exactly what Alex was determined to avoid.

Cassie jammed her hands in her pockets and trudged toward the trailer. Sneaking around might work for a while but she wouldn't be happy for long. It was crazy to even consider it. They'd both end up empty and bitter.

And then poor Grace would be soured by three angry adults.

The cheery driver stepped from the cab, a clipboard in his hand. She forced a return smile and initialed the shipping papers, then stood back while he lowered the ramp.

He led Freckles off the trailer and passed her the rope. "Horse traveled like a pro," the driver said. "I didn't even know he was back there."

"Great," she said, giving Freckles a welcoming pat. He looked around with pricked ears, curious but unafraid.

She waited until the truck and trailer disappeared down the driveway, then led Freckles around the yard, introducing him to his new home and letting him stretch his legs. The horse ambled beside her, as relaxed as he'd been yesterday at the Center.

Gramps stepped down from the verandah, the blue ribbon in his hand. "We've had some wild ones here," he said, studying Freckles with a knowledgeable eye. "That horse is definitely not one of them."

"He's used to the commotion of a movie set," she said. "He'll be perfect for Grace."

"I'll take off his shipping bandages," Gramps said. He passed her the ribbon and crouched down to remove the wraps. "Tie that ribbon around his neck so it's on when they get here. I called Alex and they're on their way."

Cassie stared at the ribbon clutched in her hand. She'd been hoping for a little more time before she saw Alex. Panic roiled with her hurt and she didn't know what to say, or even what to think.

She fastened the cheery ribbon around Freckles' neck. The color was a bit faded but the words were big and clear:

CONGRATS ON YOUR NEW HORSE! The first time she'd seen the ribbon had been when Alex had mischievously wrapped it around an outlaw horse sent for training. She wasn't sure how he'd even managed to get close enough to fasten it around the crazy animal's neck.

The stallion had been tearing around the round pen, biting and kicking at the rails, furious at his confinement. It was obvious he was going to be a dangerous ride, the type where your heart jammed in your throat and you only prayed you'd be stepping from the saddle under your own steam.

She'd just started playing polo and she didn't want to break any more bones. And while the ribbon had been a great joke her smile had wobbled. But she hadn't wanted to swallow her pride and admit to her grandfather that she was a little bit afraid. And she certainly didn't want Gramps to have to ride a crazy horse like that.

Alex had studied her for a moment. His grin had faded and he'd turned to Gramps. "I'd like to ride this one, sir," he said. "That horse reminds me of one my dad used to own."

As if his father had ever allowed dangerous untrained horses in the fancy Sutherland stables. But Alex had always protected her. Never let anyone, or anything hurt her. Except him.

And she had no defenses against him. She gripped Freckles' lead rope a little tighter, her palms sweaty. She had to get out of here. Away from Alex and his knowing eyes, and those hands that could sweep away her good intentions and make her burn with longing.

They knew each other too well. She'd probably never love anyone else the way she loved him. But she needed the chance to make a new life. To have a family of her own. That wouldn't happen if she stayed here, waiting around for him.

So there was really no decision. She'd have to ask Alex and Grace to stay away until she sold the horses. And then she'd convince Gramps to come with her. They could make another home somewhere, and never come back.

Alex wouldn't pursue her. He'd already demonstrated that. He only cared about keeping his life with Rachel completely tranquil.

Well, he could find another instructor for Grace. Another woman to sneak on his plane. Because it would hurt too much to live off crumbs, content with his padded wallet and leftover affection. However, a little sigh escaped and Freckles turned his head, eyeing her with concern.

"Sorry, fellow," she said. "It's all right. Everything's okay." But her voice cracked and deep down she didn't think anything would ever be okay again.

♦

Alex eased up on the gas pedal, maneuvering around a beeping yellow paving truck. A crew was already out repairing potholes. Soon this back road would be much smoother, which would cut down his driving time by at least five minutes. Every second with Cassie mattered. They had to grab their time whenever they could.

She'd been so quiet when he dropped her off last night. Obviously she hadn't liked the plane idea but he'd already worked up a new proposal. One he hoped would suit her better.

Grace perched in the passenger's seat, fiddling with his

file folder.

"What's the surprise, Dad?" She opened the file and stared at the papers on her lap. "Are you buying a new farm?"

"That's not the surprise," he said. "Close the file, please."

"Is this place for sale?" she asked, still flipping through the pictures. "It looks nice. It has a barn and lake and lots of nice places to ride."

"Put it away, Grace," he said, more firmly this time.

She gave a long-suffering sigh but closed the folder. "I'm glad Cassie's back," she said. "I missed not having my lesson yesterday. Mom asked where you were. And if you two went somewhere together."

"Did you have fun with her and Santiago?" he asked, keeping his voice light.

"I guess," Grace said. "But Mom and I are both happier when you're around. And she was arguing a lot with Santiago. She thinks one of the kittens is sick."

Dread chilled Alex's chest. "Which one?" he asked.

"The little kitten that I'm keeping, you know, Socks. I wanted to call the vet but Mom said you'd know how to make her better."

Alex turned so numb he hit the jagged rut marking the entrance of Jake Edwards' driveway. The Benz jolted in protest. He bit back his curse, hoping he wouldn't get a flat. He would have preferred to grab the Volvo for these rough drives but Grace liked the convertible. And fortunately the car continued to move smoothly.

"Is the surprise here?" Grace asked, leaning forward with fresh interest. "Did Mr. Edwards get a new horse I can groom?"

Grace didn't ask for much, he thought bleakly. Just a horse she could brush...and for him to stick around and keep her safe from her damn mother. Surely Cassie could understand that.

"There is a new horse here," he said, easing the car to a stop behind the barn. "But you can do more than brush him."

She stared for a moment, her eyes wide. Then she whipped open the passenger door and scrambled out before he had time to cut the engine.

She bolted into the barn but reappeared in seconds, her face confused. "There's no horse inside," she said. "Only Ginger. Are you teasing? What did you mean? Is it my new horse?"

"Let's walk around the barn," he said.

They rounded the barn and Grace jerked to a halt. Cassie and Jake stood beside Freckles. Both of them were grinning, and a huge ribbon fluttered around Freckles' shiny neck. Grace stared at the words on the ribbon, then at the horse, her eyes widening. Then she rushed up, wrapped her arms around Freckles and burst into tears.

Freckles stood stock still, as if accustomed to theatrical young girls crying and hanging onto his neck. And maybe he was.

"Thank you, D-dad," Grace said. "Is he really mine? Thank you, Cassie and Mr. Edwards." Her words ran together and she planted ecstatic kisses on Freckles' nose. "He's so beautiful. What's his name? Can I ride him?"

Alex looked at Cassie but she avoided his gaze. She was smiling at Grace, outwardly relaxed. But her mouth was tight, her shoulders a little too straight. She looked the same as she did last night, when she'd brushed off his good-night kiss and bolted from the car.

"What do you think, Cass?" he asked. "Can Grace ride him? Or does Freckles need time to settle?"

Cassie didn't answer, instead seemed preoccupied with re-coiling the lead rope. However, Jake grinned, oblivious to the tension. Clearly he shared Grace's sentiments and thought her new horse was the most exciting thing in the world.

"The horse's name is Freckles," Jake said, his voice booming. "And of course you can ride him. He's very sensible. Grab your helmet and your dad can boost you up."

Grace jumped in glee and had her helmet buckled on in seconds. And then Jake was leading Freckles around the barnyard, and Grace was alternating between squeals of joy and leaning forward and hugging her new horse's neck.

Alex kept his eyes on Grace but every other sense was locked on Cassie. He pulled in a frustrated breath, remembering how good it had felt to be with her again. To hear her little sighs when he was moving deep inside her. The sheer joy of having her back in his life. And he wanted that, permanently. They were too good together to give it up.

He folded his arms over his chest, fighting the urge to drop to his knees and beg. Grace and Jake were so busy with Freckles they probably wouldn't even notice. But having her last night was like opening a floodgate. He needed her. In his bed, in his day, in his life. Clearly she hadn't liked the plane idea, but a property would make more sense. He should have known she'd prefer ground beneath her feet.

He'd put the deed in her name, a hundred acres, sixteen-stall barn and, as Grace had noted, it even had a small lake. Cassie and her grandfather could tinker around all they wanted. He'd keep an employee on hand, someone to look after repairs who could double as a watchman...just in case.

With time, Rachel would accept things. She'd have to.

"I need a favor," Cassie said. She smiled and waved back at Grace who hadn't stopped beaming and waving every time she and Freckles circled the barn.

"Anything," Alex said gruffly.

"The college won't try out Gramps' horses unless Santiago approves them. He's already ridden Ginger but we have three more polo ponies. So it would help if he'd come over here and give them a fair trial."

"Certainly," he said. "I'll talk to Santiago today."

"Thank you." She didn't say anything else but it was a good sign that she was asking something of him, even if it wasn't much of a favor. Unless it meant that she just wanted to sell the horses and move both her and her grandfather out of state. And his relief fizzled.

"I didn't mean to offend you with the plane idea," he said cautiously. "And I apologize. But I talked to my realtor this morning. There are some nice places on the market, within an hour's drive. One in particular looks perfect. You could do some training there, or teaching. Stay involved with horses, just like you always wanted—"

"Would you live there?" she asked, her voice sad.

"You know I can't," he said. "Not unless I have sole custody of Grace."

"Then why don't you get it? Can't you pay off Rachel? You said she only cares about money."

"I've tried, many times." He clamped his mouth shut. Didn't want to admit that his elite team of lawyers hadn't yet been able to entice her. He'd even offered to void the prenup and split all assets. She'd refused, saying emotional turbulence wasn't good for her...or Grace. Three weeks later, Grace had stopped eating.

"Rachel has issues," he said, clearing his throat. He didn't like to talk about this to anyone, even the therapists, but he'd never kept secrets from Cassie. And she needed to know. Needed to understand. "She cut me once," he admitted, his hand drifting over his rib. "She's better now, but I don't trust her with Grace."

Cassie's eyes widened. She didn't speak. She just looked stunned. "Oh," she said slowly. "That scar?"

He nodded, hating his helplessness.

"But she's bound to find out about any plane rides or secret acreages on the other side of town," Cassie said. "And we can't endanger Grace. Or you." Her saw her swallow, then raise a brave chin. He knew that look. It meant she'd made a decision and it wasn't one he'd like.

"Trust me, Cass," he said, fighting his panic. "I'll think of something. But I can't let Rachel twist Grace up, just to get back at me. You have to understand."

"Oh, I understand," Cassie said. She crossed her arms and edged a step away, and it was clear she didn't want him around. Not today. Maybe not tomorrow either. And he couldn't even fault her thinking.

Rachel was a time bomb and the estate, though big, could never hold them all. Rachel presided over it like it was her family property, and then played Grace like a puppet.

She'd never stop. Never change.

And as he stared at Cassie's beloved face, a calm resignation swept him. And he knew what had to be done. Rachel was too ruthless, too wily and altogether too dangerous. He needed her out of Grace's life. And Cassie's. It was regrettable that it had come to this, but Rachel was his mistake to fix. And he couldn't risk losing the two people he loved most.

"Just give me a little more time," he said, hating the thickness of his throat, the regret he couldn't hide. "I'll make Rachel another offer. One I'm positive she'll like."

But Cassie was busy waving at Grace and didn't appear to hear. Or perhaps she simply wasn't comforted by his words. And why would she be?

He'd failed her before. Words didn't mean much to her, and he wasn't very good with them. So this time he'd have to show her with action.

CHAPTER TWENTY-SIX

"Freckles is so wonderful, Daddy," Grace said, still bouncing on the passenger's seat. She hadn't stopped grinning since she led Freckles into his stall and kissed the horse good night. "I wish we didn't have to go home. Did you see me trotting? He didn't buck or anything, and he stopped whenever I asked."

Her teeth flashed in a buoyant smile, and she looked happier than he'd ever seen her. "Thank you for buying him," she went on. "I'm going to keep him forever. And he's not a pony so I won't get too big. He's just as tall as Digger, almost, but I'm not going to ever wear spurs. And I don't want Mom to ride him, okay?"

Alex gave an affirming nod. He didn't want Rachel riding Freckles either. But there was little danger of that. Freckles was a people pleaser, but he wasn't a credentialed polo pony. Rachel would consider it demeaning to sit on such a horse.

"I sent Mom some pictures," Grace said, staring down at her phone. "But she sometimes takes a long time to answer."

"What pictures did you send?" he asked, keeping his voice calm, careful to hide his alarm.

"Two of me riding, one of him eating a peppermint and rolling his lip, and another of me braiding his mane."

"So just pictures of you and him?"

Grace gave an agreeable nod. "And one with Cassie," she added.

He gripped the steering wheel. Rachel was jealous of any woman he spent time with, but she'd always harbored a special animosity toward Cassie. Had sensed the depth of his feelings.

A text pinged. Grace stared down at the phone, still smiling. But her smile faded as she scanned the message. "Oh, no! One of the kittens is missing." Her lower lip trembled, and it was clear she was struggling not to cry.

A muscle twitched in Alex's jaw. It always hurt to see her like this. She'd been so happy, playing like a carefree kid at Jake's barn. And now she was reduced to tears. Rachel had never shown any scruples but this was abhorrent. He didn't even need to ask which kitten was missing. It would be Socks, of course. Grace's favorite, and the one she'd planned to keep.

"We're almost home," he said. "I'm sure I'll be able to find the kitten."

"I don't know how Socks got out of the stall. Maybe she was really sick and crawled off somewhere." And now sobs punctuated Grace's words. "Mom was right. I should have stayed home. Then this would never have happened."

His knuckles whitened around the wheel. He could handle Rachel trying to control him but not when her ruthlessness extended to Grace. The past year had been relatively smooth but Cassie's return had fueled her vindictiveness. The woman didn't deserve to be a mother.

Gravel crunched beneath his tires, silencing as he turned onto the smooth pavement of the long drive. His mind whirled. He truly loved this place, would hate to give up the estate. But he loved Grace and Cassie more.

He took the quicker servants' entrance and eased to a stop in front of the poolhouse. "You get out here. I'll go find your kitten."

"But I want to help."

"The housekeeper has supper ready," he said. "And she'll help you search around the orchard. That way a larger area is covered, in case the kitten wandered away from the barn."

Grace nibbled at her lip. Then she nodded agreement, eased from the car and trudged toward the house. Earlier she'd been laughing and smiling, calling this the best day ever. But her special day had just come to a screeching halt.

Now there was no need to hide his fury. He whipped the convertible in a circle and sped to the barn. Stepped out and slammed the door with a crack.

Rachel's car was there but the paddocks were empty. All the horses were settled in their stalls for the night which meant the grooms had returned to their quarters. There'd be no one else around to witness his anger. He didn't give a damn about appearances anyway, only so much as it affected Grace.

He stalked into the barn, so taut he could feel a muscle pulsing in his jaw.

Rachel sat in a chair in front of the office, as if awaiting his arrival. The aisle lights spotlighted her sleek golden hair. Her legs were crossed in an elegant pose, outlining the curves of her shapely legs. The first time he'd seen her sashaying into class, every male in the class had drooled. Now he knew the warped mind beneath her beautiful veneer and he couldn't keep his mouth from twisting with revulsion.

"Where's Grace's kitten?" he snapped.

"Oh, my," she said mockingly. "Don't look so affronted. Do you really think you can hang out with your old girlfriend with no retaliation?"

"We're divorced, Rachel. And your malicious games aren't hurting me. They're hurting Grace."

"Who we both know is the only way I can hurt you." Her smile was triumphant, and chilling. "We can live in harmony and I'll be good to Grace. But only if you promise not to see that slut again."

He folded his arms, fighting the urge to pick her up from the chair and shake some sense into her.

She rose and stepped forward, standing so close he could smell her spitefulness. "You want to kill me, don't you?"

"Sometimes," he said.

"You should know I'm recording this conversation."

"Which will be carefully edited, I'm sure."

"Of course it will. You're not the only one with good lawyers."

"I've never edited anything," he said. "I don't have to. And I have enough ammo to end up with custody."

"Maybe. But that will take time. In the meantime Grace needs and wants her mother. Do you really want to be responsible when she becomes anorexic again? Because you know I can make that happen, just like I did before. Or even worse. How would you feel if she started cutting her arms—?"

His vision blurred, spotted by black dots of anger. He jerked forward and wrapped his hands around her arms, hating to touch her. Unable not to.

Rachel shot him a victorious smile. Then she let out an anguished scream. "You're hurting me," she whimpered. "Please don't hit me. Not again."

"Oh, for God's sake." He loosened his hands and stepped back, shaking his head in disgust, as annoyed by his lack of control as he was at her calculated staging. He'd lived with her stunts for years. He shouldn't be surprised.

"This is how it's going to work," Rachel said, her voice hardening. "I'll be the dutiful mother you want for your daughter, but don't ever flaunt your women in my face. The only way you'll get rid of me is with a hit man. And we both know I'd leave enough evidence to convict you...and Grace would have to live the rest of her life as an orphan."

He gave his head a weary shake. "You honestly don't give a damn, do you?" Deep down he hoped she harbored some affection for Grace, some sort of warmth for the child she'd carried.

"I love you," Rachel said. "And you're Grace's father. So of course I love her."

He backed up, not wanting to even breathe the same air. He'd deluded himself into thinking Rachel was just selfish like his parents. That he could help keep her psychosis in check. But it was apparent she had no real affection for Grace.

"Don't look at me like that," Rachel said. "We're in this together. For life."

For life. Bile rose in his throat. "Return Grace's kitten," he said tiredly. "Unharmed."

"Of course," Rachel said mockingly. "The puny little kitten with the white feet. I wanted to toss her in the pool but Santiago is surprisingly soft. Turns out he likes cats. You're lucky he was here." She waved a dismissive hand then pressed a number on her phone.

"Grace, darling," she purred. "I found your kitten. It took me hours but she's safe and sound. I'll be in later to kiss you good night."

He could hear Grace's whoop of joy but Rachel cut the connection while Grace was still talking.

"See," Rachel said, palming her diamond encrusted phone. "I know how to make little Grace happy. And I can do the same for you. Just like I did before." She sidled closer, trailing suggestive fingers down his forearm. "Remember the things I did to you. How I took you in my mouth and made you moan…"

After Cassie's wholesome sweetness, her touch felt like insects running over his skin, and he flinched.

Her eyes glittered and she dropped her hand. "So you're already screwing her again. How convenient. Just like your horn dog father. Dropping off your kid so you can indulge in some private riding of your own."

He didn't answer. What he shared with Cassie was infinitely precious. Just the thought of her left him feeling cleaner, happier, more alive. And it only underscored that he had to free himself from Rachel, no matter the cost.

"What do you want, Rachel?" he asked.

"Everything," she said. "And I will never let any woman share this estate with you. It's mine, all of it. I wish you'd understand that."

"I do." He inclined his head. "So my lawyers will be contacting you with a new proposal."

And with that he turned and walked away.

"Wait," she called. "Remember I'll never leave the estate. So you can't win. Not if you want your daughter safe, happy…"

She was still yelling, making the wide-eyed horses flinch in their stalls, when he escaped outside into the blessedly fresh air.

CHAPTER TWENTY-SEVEN

"You heard correctly," Alex said, calmly eyeing the senior partner of the Dyer Law Firm, a company that had ably represented generations of Sutherlands in both their personal and business affairs. "In addition to half the assets, Rachel can have the estate and all the contents, including the horses. But I want the cats."

His lawyer blanched. "A million dollars worth of horseflesh and you're fighting for some barn cats?"

"She can have everything. But start with the estate and forty percent of the Sutherland holdings. Bottom line is she has to give up parental rights, immediately."

"I advise against relinquishing the property. Let me move some assets and then we can dangle more money. And you need to think a little longer about this."

Alex shook his head. He didn't want to think about his home: the mansion with three curving staircases that Cassie had used as her personal slides, the poolhouse where Grace had learned to walk, and the pristine fields he and Cassie had raced across. He'd never offered Rachel free and clear title before. Never thought he could bear to give up the family estate. But yesterday she'd done the unthinkable—she'd threatened Grace—and his belief about what was best for his daughter had dramatically shifted.

"I want this done now." Alex leaned back in the chair and adopted a languid pose. "She's always wanted the estate. Give it to her."

"But your parents would be horrified. The Sutherland family—

"It's okay," he said quietly, almost gently. "Just do it."

The lawyer gave a ponderous sigh, picked up a gold fountain pen and scrawled a notation. "We'll talk to her legal representation and draw up the papers. I'll request that she sign within twenty-four hours." He adjusted his glasses, eyeing Alex hopefully. "Sure you don't want to reconsider?"

Alex shook his head. For nine years he'd struggled to make this work, considering it his duty to do what was right for Grace, and Rachel. He'd accepted that he could never trust her to look after Grace, but he hadn't thought it ethical to completely sever a mother from her child. Now he had no choice.

Cassie rushed down the barn aisle and grabbed the bale of hay before her grandfather could bend down and pick it up. "Let me get the hay," she said.

He scowled and for a moment it seemed he'd argue. Then he gave a resigned shrug and stepped back. "Sometimes I forget I'm not supposed to lift," he said. "Thanks for coming home to help. Putting your life on hold."

"You don't need to thank me," she said. "I love you."

"Even though I wasn't the best guardian for a little girl? A little girl who's all grown up now." His voice thickened and there was an odd sheen to his eyes.

"Oh, Gramps." She forgot about the hay and gave him an impulsive hug, rather surprised when he awkwardly squeezed her back. He'd never been big on showing affection and his physical demonstrations had been brief and memorable.

But she remembered how he used to feel, and beneath the faded shirt his shoulders seemed smaller. In fact they felt narrow, frail and terrifyingly bony. She had to get him eating more, make some higher-calorie meals. Maybe the type of casseroles that Alex had brought.

"You gave me a home," she said. "And the best childhood a kid could ever have." And now it was her voice that sounded thick.

"But you had too many chores," he said. "And I wanted you to ride too many problem horses. You were always working."

"I loved my life here. All I ever wanted was to work with horses. You know that."

"I took your courage for granted though. You climbed on any animal, never complaining. Seeing Grace here, I realize how young you were. I didn't give you time to play."

"But Alex and I played all the time."

Gramps edged back and she dropped her arms.

"Thank God he was around," her grandfather muttered. "He looked out for you in a way I didn't. Threatened to take his lessons elsewhere if I didn't ease up. He may have been young but he always knew what was right."

She hooked her fingers around the twine of the hay bale. Yes, Alex did what was right and those fiercely protective instincts were in full force with Grace. But it hurt that he wanted to set Cassie up as a pseudo mistress. If Rachel found out, she'd be furious.

She gulped, remembered Alex's scar. He'd asked for more time to deal with Rachel but Cassie didn't want her presence to endanger anyone. And she had no idea how he would negotiate with such a woman.

She positioned the bale in front of Freckles' stall. Grace was coming over for a lesson this morning, and she liked to feed the horses plenty of hay. No doubt, a new horse would warrant extra.

"It's nice having Alex around again," Gramps said. "I lost my temper before. Told him to leave us alone. But I didn't expect him to stay away so long. When that man makes a promise, he sticks to it."

Cassie shifted the bale another inch, moving it to the left of the stall door. She didn't like this line of talk, didn't want to be reminded about Alex and his tough decisions. And she didn't want to agonize about what might happen between him and Rachel.

"I should have relented and called him," Gramps went on. "But I missed you." He gave a little chuckle. "And it wasn't because you were such a good worker."

"I had to leave," she said. "The equine center made me a great offer. I never would have found that kind of horse job here." And it would have been torture watching Alex with Rachel. And his new baby.

"It was good of Alex to recommend you. But it pissed me off. I guessed that he had hurt you but I didn't want you to move. Didn't think you'd be happy anywhere else."

She froze, her mind sluggish. What was Gramps saying?

"But it was a friend of your vet who knew about the job," she said slowly.

"Alex was the friend," her grandfather admitted. "He was the one who knew the owner. But then you moved further away with the movie work. I didn't expect that. I don't think he did either."

Her grandfather's mouth was still moving but a drumming noise filled her ears. She dropped onto the hay bale, her knees weak. So it had been Alex all along. He was the one who didn't want her living here. Didn't want her around his pregnant fiancée. So he'd shipped her out like an unwanted horse.

She'd been so relieved to land a job at the prestigious Center. So proud when she proved she could handle their wildest horses. It had led to her job in California. But she'd thought she had earned it on her own. While Alex had really been the one pulling strings.

She slumped back against the wall, mortified at how she'd guided him around the Center, showing him the technologies, introducing him to her friends, to Wally. And that explained why Wally knew Grace's age. Because Alex already knew those people.

When he'd first told her about Rachel's pregnancy, she'd been shattered. Vowed she never wanted to see him again, even though they both knew that would be impossible. They both rode at the polo club. She worked for the Sutherlands, a job that obviously was in jeopardy. But of course he'd handled it just like he dealt with everything else—quickly, efficiently and with a certain degree of ruthlessness.

She really shouldn't be annoyed. If she had stayed, she might have turned to her high school boyfriend for solace. She could have six kids and live a stone's throw from Gramps, forever in the shadow of the Sutherland Estate.

But I'd be teaching lessons to my own children now, instead of Grace. I'd be happy... Maybe.

She clasped her hands together, struggling with her ambivalence. Alex had only made the job available. He hadn't forced her to accept. And if she hadn't taken it, she never would have met Dan Barrett. Never would have been offered a position in the movie industry.

But why couldn't Alex be tough like that with Rachel? Why didn't he just offer his ex-wife a ranch and polo team in Argentina...or even further, Australia?

She gripped her fingers more tightly. Because then Grace would move too, or at least be gone for visits. Alex didn't trust Rachel with Grace, even for short periods. And rightly so.

"Tired?" her grandfather asked, sitting down on the bale beside her. "You rode three horses and mucked out all the stalls. And it's not even nine o'clock yet."

"I wanted them cleaned before Grace arrived for her lesson," Cassie said, still numb. "She wants to swing a mallet today. From Freckles' back."

She thought Gramps might protest that Grace wasn't a good enough rider, but he only nodded. Naturally he wanted to keep the Sutherlands happy. Grace's lesson money was their sole income. And if the girl wanted to swing a mallet, who were they to tell her she wasn't ready?

"I'll make sure she rides Freckles in a halter," Cassie said. "So she doesn't hurt his mouth by accident. But she's in a hurry to learn polo. She's looks up to her mother and wants to impress her."

Gramps snorted. "Rachel doesn't worry about hurting anything. Look what she did to Ginger. But we're lucky it wasn't worse."

"What do you mean?"

Gramps shrugged. "After Alex and Rachel divorced, a few women were rumored to be interested in him. Something unlucky always seemed to happen."

Cassie leaned forward on the hay bale. Gramps was not a man to gossip, or exaggerate, and 'something unlucky' seemed a euphemistic statement, even for him. Maybe there was more than the knife incident with Alex.

"You're saying Rachel...does stuff?" Her voice lowered even though the barn was empty. And while the idea was repugnant, it was no longer shocking. Not after Alex's admission yesterday. And she'd already guessed Ginger had been deliberately cut.

"I'm just saying some people follow a scorched earth policy," her grandfather said. "Rachel is one of them. And I don't believe Grace looks up to her mother. I think the kid is terrified."

Cassie blinked. Gramps had spent a lifetime studying body language. He always knew when a horse was stubborn, scared or just confused. And his assessment of Rachel wasn't surprising. But he must be wrong about Grace.

She did speak rather carefully for a nine-year-old, and her enunciation was painfully deliberate. However, Cassie had assumed that was her upbringing. Alex had been careful with his words too, almost guarded. Except around her.

But if Grace were really afraid of her mother, she hid it well. As if she wanted to conceal it from everyone. Most especially her father. Who was bending over backwards to keep the family unit together.

"Have you mentioned that to Alex?" Cassie asked.

"Of course not," Gramps said. "I can criticize his riding or his horses but he's never tolerated any comments about his family. You might be able to say something though. He's always been open with you—"

"No, I can't. Not now." She jerked to her feet. Rachel was already a hot topic. And Cassie was hurting too much, feeling far too fragile. It was like they were poised over a precipice with both her and Alex desperately trying to find a solution.

"Besides," she said, "Grace adores her mother. Everything she does is for her. She always wants to impress her. To please."

Her grandfather gave a stubborn shake of his head. "That's because she's scared," he said.

CHAPTER TWENTY-EIGHT

"Lean further over his shoulder when you swing," Cassie called, walking toward the middle of the field so she'd be closer to Grace and Freckles. "Just make sure you don't hit his legs."

Grace leaned over the saddle, concentration evident in the set of her chin. She pulled back her mallet and swung. There was a satisfying crack and the ball bounced over the grass. Grace whooped with triumph and even Freckles appeared pleased, his eyes tracking the ball as it rolled down the field.

"Well done!" Cassie called, her voice lifting with excitement. "Now trot to the ball and hit it again."

Freckles seemed to understand the directions. He pricked his ears and trotted after the ball, even approaching from the left as if aware his rider held the mallet in her right hand. He was remarkably helpful, positioning himself for the swing and remaining rock solid until Grace's seat was safely back in the saddle.

There were no control issues from riding him in a halter either. He wasn't trying to take advantage of the fact that he had no bit in his mouth, or that his rookie rider wasn't giving him much guidance.

Grace hit the ball again and it trickled across the goal line.

"I did it" she called, pumping her mallet in the air. "I love this game. I love this horse!"

Cassie laughed. Freckles wasn't at all concerned about the mallet waving so close to his face. He was fearless, the type of horse determined to do a good job no matter the task. And he inspired confidence in Grace, who was now leaning forward and hitting the ball with the gusto of a more advanced player. The groundwork they'd done with the mallet had also helped. She wasn't missing many balls.

Grace trotted back to Cassie, a grin splitting her face. She pulled Freckles to a stop and showered him with neck pats. "He's following the ball by himself. How does he know to do that?"

"He thinks like a cowhorse," Cassie said. "Except he's working the ball, not a steer." She set the bucket of balls on the grass. "Freckles is taking great care of you. Maybe you should reward him now. For the movies, we give the animals a break every hour."

"I'll get off now," Grace said quickly. "Loosen his girth and let him eat some grass in the shade. Then afterwards maybe we can practice some more?"

Cassie gave an approving nod. Grace might be heir to billions but she definitely knew to take care of her horse. It had taken Gramps time to teach Alex that same lesson. When his father had first dropped him off, Alex had viewed horses as machines, questioning why Cassie was always trying to find shade.

"You don't even own most of these horses," he'd said. "They're just at your grandfather's for training."

"They still get hot," she said, squeezing her horse behind the barn, on the tiny strip of shaded ground where her grandfather always took his riding breaks. "Gramps says to treat them firmly but with kindness and respect. Then they'll try harder."

Alex had just rolled his eyes and sauntered into the kitchen to grab a glass of water. But the next week he found some old boards and a tarp, and made a bigger overhang against the outer wall of the barn. After that there was room for three horses and they always had the perfect spot to stand and take a break.

It was sometimes hard to analyze his reasons but once he decided on a course of action, he always followed it. He'd certainly taught Grace to take good care of her animals. For some reason, Grace just hadn't enjoyed riding...until now. So maybe Gramps was right and the girl really did fear her mother.

Cassie pulled two bottles of water from the bucket and followed Grace to the tree line. The girl had already dismounted and was loosening her girth, crooning to Freckles the entire time. She might be reserved like Alex but fortunately she'd also inherited his innate kindness, not Rachel's mercenary nature.

Freckles lowered his head to grab bites of grass, as if aware he was being rewarded with free time and considered it his due.

"It's good he already has a halter on," Grace said. "It's easier for him to chew without a bit in his mouth. I won't be able to do this when I take him home though. Mom doesn't let her horses eat grass when they're saddled. And I really want her to like him."

"She will," Cassie said, passing Grace a bottle of water. "But it's fun to hang out with your horse and take grass breaks together. It builds a bond."

"At our stable the grooms hold the horses," Grace said.

"And Mom and Santiago take their breaks in the office."

Of course, Cassie thought, twisting the cap off her water bottle. The Sutherland barn had an air-conditioned lounge with a full kitchen and bar. The office was similarly equipped, but located at the back and much more private. Rachel and Santiago clearly spent a lot of time together. Maybe if Rachel had a new boyfriend she'd give up her fixation on Alex, and it wouldn't be necessary to spend time on a plane or live miles apart in a secret house.

She sipped her water, picturing Santiago. She'd only met him that one day at the Club but he was definitely handsome with striking dark features and an athletic build. No doubt, women found the star player attractive. But there had been something in his eyes, a careful watchfulness that had been rather disconcerting. Of course, she and Gramps had been upset about Ginger, more or less accusing Santiago of going back on his word. Naturally the man had been displeased.

"How long has Santiago ridden for your mom?" Cassie asked, stepping forward and swatting a stubborn horsefly off Freckles' rump.

"About two years," Grace said. "Mom met him at a tournament in Florida. He really helps the team and they've been winning a lot more since he came. The last trophy was so nice Mom put it in the display case. She's getting so good at polo."

At usual Grace talked more about her mother's abilities than her father. She didn't seem to realize Alex was much more accomplished. But where did Santiago fit in? Maybe he was the one who intimidated Grace. It sounded like she had stopped riding about two years ago, about the same time Santiago had arrived. And Grace had refused to take a lesson from him when Cassie had been away at the Center. Maybe it wasn't fear but simple aversion.

Cassie pressed her lips together, loath to pump a student for information. She sat down, trying to focus instead on counting the polo balls in the bucket. It was a luxury to have so many. Seven were scattered in the grass behind the goal posts but those could be retrieved at the end of the lesson. That was another fun thing Grace could do with Freckles. Gather balls. A nice safe activity, away from Santiago.

And then she couldn't keep her mouth shut any longer. Because if Grace was afraid of Santiago, there was probably good reason. And Cassie couldn't ignore it. "Do you hang out in the office too?" she asked. "With your mom and Santiago?"

"No," Grace said. "Mom and Santiago need to talk, and plan their game plays in private. So I help the grooms. Sometimes they let me bandage if a horse is quiet enough."

Cassie's gaze turned to Freckles' legs. It was standard to wrap a horse's legs to protect against swinging mallets. And Grace had done an excellent job bandaging. The polo wraps were snug and even. "Did your mother teach you how to wrap?" she asked.

"Oh, no," Grace said, her eyes widening. "Mom doesn't do that. Grooms take care of that stuff. That's why we pay them. And then polo creates jobs for the ones who can't afford horses. Mom is really nice about helping people like that." But her words sounded hollow and she shot Cassie an odd look. "You think Mom's nice, right?"

"Of course." Cassie fingered the handle of the bucket, afraid Grace had caught something in her expression. "Your mom is definitely a hard-working polo player," she added, searching for something positive to say. "Very committed. I worked as a groom at your stable when she was in college. Your dad brought her back to play sometimes. She practiced all day."

"In New York she never had good horses to ride," Grace said. "But after she met Dad, she was able to ride on better teams. And have better polo ponies. It's important to play to win. Especially when people are watching."

Grace bent and plucked a daisy. She rolled the stem between her fingers then slowly pulled off each pedal. She didn't say anything else and the only sound was of Freckles chomping grass.

Grace stared a long moment at her hand. Then she abruptly opened her fingers, letting the mutilated flower fall to the ground. "That's why she doesn't want me to ride," she said tonelessly. "Because I'm fat. And people will see. She's embarrassed I'm not very good. And that I'll take up too much of Dad's time."

Cassie gaped, swept with anger and an aching empathy. *Rachel didn't want Grace to ride? And Grace knew it?*

"But it'll be different with Freckles," Grace went on. "She'll finally be proud of me. And maybe it'll even be fun again."

Cassie jerked to her feet so fast she knocked over the bucket of balls. This was definitely abuse, emotional abuse of the worst kind. "You should talk to your dad about this."

"No! He'll just get angry at Mom. And I don't want him to leave."

"Your dad won't leave you," Cassie said, blinking in dismay.

"Yes, he will. And then I'll have to move to Argentina with Mom and Santiago, and I'll never see him again."

"So you'd rather live with your dad?"

"I want to live with them both." Grace twisted at her hands, her face flushed with emotion. "I want everything to stay exactly like it is now," she said. "And I want to talk about a different subject, please."

"Okay," Cassie said, her heart aching for the young girl. "How about I get a horse and we pass the ball back and forth? See how Freckles behaves in a game situation."

"That will be nice. But please don't tell Mom I was talking about her. Or Santiago when he comes."

"Santiago?" Cassie asked, her head still spinning from Grace's revelation. "Is he coming here?"

"Yes," Grace said. "I heard Dad tell him to drive over here and check out your horses today. They were talking low though, so I couldn't hear everything."

Probably whispering so no one would hear. Rachel definitely wouldn't like the idea of her right-hand man fraternizing with the enemy. No doubt Santiago would be displeased as well—forced to drive to Gramps' rundown property and evaluate some horses, instead of lounging in an air-conditioned office, flirting with Rachel.

Didn't matter though, because Alex's word was law. And with Santiago's approval, Gramps would have a chance at selling to the collegiate team. Santiago would have to judge the horses as suitable...if he were honest. At least he was coming here to ride and would be removed from Rachel's influence.

Gramps would be ecstatic with this news. Cassie just hoped Santiago would give them a fair trial. And that she'd have a chance to tell Alex about his daughter's reluctant disclosure.

CHAPTER TWENTY-NINE

Cassie cringed as Santiago leaned down and took another belly shot, fearlessly swinging his mallet between Digger's churning legs. She peeked at her grandfather, checking his reaction. It was great that Santiago had come today, but her grandfather had never condoned high risk shots. And to possibly lame a horse Santiago didn't own seemed rather irresponsible...unless he was acting on Rachel's instructions.

However her grandfather didn't make a sound. He simply crossed his arms and looked stoic. He'd insisted on walking down to the south field to watch, but now she wished he'd remained on the porch. This was simply too important. If Santiago liked the horses, the college would reconsider their purchase. Heck, even if he just liked one of them, it would provide Gramps with some income. It would also be one less horse to feed, one less animal for him to worry about.

"Digger sure looks different with Santiago riding," Grace said. "I didn't realize he could run so fast."

Cassie nodded, deciding she needed to be more grateful. Alex had kindly asked Santiago to come, and the man was here. No doubt about it, Santiago was a superb rider. He was giving quite a show. Digger zipped around the field, responding instantly to his rider's commands. He wasn't as fast as Ginger but he was agile and gallant, and not at all intimidated by Santiago's mallet swinging so close to his fragile legs.

"I thought you didn't allow belly shots on your horses," Grace said. She lowered her voice even though Santiago was galloping at the far end of the field.

"They're okay if you're a pro," Cassie said, trying to be diplomatic. "And Santiago has excellent timing."

But Gramps gave a derisive snort. "A millionaire's shot," he said. "The only people that try those are the rich. Because they don't care about crippling up their horses."

"But Mom tries those shots all the time," Grace said.

"Exactly," Gramps said.

Cassie gave him a quick nudge, suspecting everything they said would be repeated to Rachel. "Digger and Santiago both look great out there," she said, changing the subject. "They're working well together. We should have shaved Digger's mane first though, like Ginger's. So it doesn't tangle up the reins."

"I suppose," Gramps said. "But other disciplines prefer a mane. I hate to cut it until I'm positive he's going to a polo home. Digger does seem to trust Santiago though. And I'm glad he came here because I refuse to let my horses go out on trial again." His voice darkened. "Not after what happened to Ginger."

"I'm going back to the barn now," Grace muttered.

She turned and retreated up the path, her shoulders hunched.

"Please don't talk about Rachel when Grace is around," Cassie said, giving her grandfather a reproachful look. "No one likes to hear negative things about their parents."

"I'm always upfront with my students," Gramps said. "With everyone. You know that. Besides, that kid already knows the truth. She's just not used to hearing it. And I'm not afraid of Rachel."

Cassie sighed. He should be afraid. Rachel had already damaged his reputation, and the only reason Santiago was here today was because of Alex. Quite likely Santiago hadn't even told Rachel that he was coming. Which meant the horses had to be approved today, before Grace went home and told her mother about his visit.

Santiago galloped a graceful loop around the goal line then cantered toward them, tall and motionless in the saddle. Usually she could tell when a rider liked a horse but his helmet shaded the top of his face, and his lower jaw was unreadable. She pressed her palms against her jeans. Felt her grandfather stiffen beside her. Despite his brave talk, he knew Santiago's approval was critical.

Santiago pulled Digger to a halt. He tugged off his helmet, and it was clear now that he was smiling. "I like this horse," he said. "He's not as fast as your mare but he's more tractable. I put him under a lot of pressure and he handled it well. He'd be a solid mount for any college team."

Cassie didn't realize she was holding her breath until it escaped in a rush of relief.

"I have two more, about the same level as him," Gramps said quickly. "I'm sure you'll like them too. Cassie can tack them up."

"No," Santiago said, shaking his head. "I don't have time to ride any more horses. It's a busy time with lots going on. Maybe in the fall."

Cassie met Gramps' gaze and the disappointment she

saw in his face mirrored her own. September would be too late. The college intended to purchase their horses by the end of the month.

Her eyes narrowed on Santiago. He was the collegiate advisor. Surely he knew their buying plans.

"The committee is in the process of making a short list," she said, studying his expression. "We'd like our horses to be on that list."

Santiago shrugged. The smile remained on his face but he adjusted the reins, avoiding her gaze. And then she understood. This was all futile. He'd come today because of Alex. But he worked for Rachel. And he wasn't about to do anything to jeopardize relations with her—whatever that relationship was.

"We can have the horses ready in minutes," Gramps said. And the plea in his voice wrenched at Cassie's heart. "They won't take long to evaluate. They're nice horses too, sound and athletic. Tex is a little green but he's almost as fast as Ginger. We'll bring them both down at the same time. I'll hurry."

He twisted toward the path but Cassie placed a hand on his arm, hating to hear her proud grandfather reduced to begging. "It's okay," she said. "Santiago knows they're nice horses. And that they'd be great for the college. But he works for someone else."

She couldn't resist shooting Santiago a hard glare. It wouldn't affect him—the man was too arrogant—but it made her feel better.

However, his reaction surprised her. He actually looked rather surprised. Then a look of resignation crossed his face. "That's right," he admitted, leaning over Digger's neck. "And the college won't buy your horses unless my boss wants it to happen. So my opinion is irrelevant. Until I have further direction, we're all just wasting time here. Yours as well as mine."

His gaze cut over her head, and he straightened in the saddle.

Cassie swung around. Alex had stepped from the path in the trees and was striding toward them. "How's it going?" he asked, stopping behind Cassie.

Santiago gave a polite nod. "I like this horse," he said. "Jake did an excellent job with his training."

"Did you try the other two yet?" Alex asked.

Santiago shook his head.

"But you're going to," Alex said, and it wasn't a question.

"Yes, of course. If that's what you want." Santiago quickly replaced his helmet. "I'll check out whatever they bring me."

"It would be easier for you to ride back to the barn," Alex said, "than for Cassie or Jake to walk. You're quite capable of tacking up a horse. We'll wait for you here."

Santiago looked at Cassie then inclined his head. She nodded back, her mouth twitching. She didn't dare look at her grandfather for fear she might laugh. And she didn't want to rouse Santiago's resentment any further. But it was enjoyable to see the man brought down a peg, even if it wouldn't help. Obviously, once Santiago reported the day's events to Rachel, the woman would do her best to scuttle any sale.

Gramps seemed to share her concern, remaining silent as Santiago rode Digger up the path to the barn. But worry lines etched his forehead.

"Did Grace have trouble with Freckles?" Alex asked. "I

was hoping to arrive in time to see her ride."

"Oh, no, she did super." Cassie swung around to look at Alex. She wasn't sure how she'd feel when she saw him today. The thought of living miles away on another acreage, risking Rachel's wrath, and then learning that he'd arranged for her job at the Center all those years ago left her conflicted. But there was no doubt his presence lifted her spirits. It always had.

"Freckles was perfectly mellow," she added. "And very obliging. At the end of the ride Grace was even hitting the ball at a trot. They're a great team."

"Then why do you two look so serious?" Alex asked, sweeping them both with a deep grin. He looked surprisingly relaxed considering their tension yesterday, and she couldn't help but smile back.

They had much to discuss and there was no need to let Rachel darken this moment. He deserved to know the horse he'd bought for his daughter was perfect and no doubt he needed a break from his complicated life, both business and personal. His expression reminded her of simpler times when they were much younger and merely excited about an upcoming show. And it was nice to see.

"It's just that Cassie and I are worried," Gramps said darkly. "Because we're not sure how unbiased Santiago will be."

Alex's smile faded and Cassie gave a mental groan.

"He won't be biased," Alex said. "At least not against you."

"What about Rachel?" Gramps asked.

"She doesn't have anything to do with the college," Alex said. "Santiago is the advisor. And it's in his interest that the team be well mounted... You can trust him."

Alex looked back at Cassie, his smile returning. "Can you tell me about Grace's ride? I planned to be here but my meeting went longer than planned."

He was more interested in hearing how his daughter had ridden with a mallet than worried about any college sale. So Cassie obliged, describing every step of Grace's ride. Gramps grew bored and wandered off to the bottom of the path, but Alex hung on her every word.

"She was really able to hit the ball at a trot?" he asked, splaying his hand around her hip. "That's wonderful, Cass. You're a great teacher."

She blinked, surprised by his casual gesture. It seemed so natural and she liked the feel of his hand. But now she understood a little more about why they needed to be secretive. And Santiago was returning soon with Tex, and Gramps was close by, pacing near the bottom of the path, anxiously awaiting his horse.

"What are you doing?" she whispered.

"What I should have done years ago." Alex's smile widened. He tugged her closer, so close she could feel the thud of his heart. Could sense his elation.

"There's no need to worry anymore," he said. "My lawyers are making Rachel a new offer. In exchange she'll be giving up all parental rights. It'll be over, Cass."

She stilled, almost lightheaded with disbelief. So she wouldn't have to agonize about what to do? What repercussions their being together might have for Grace? She and Alex wouldn't have to live apart, or fly around in a jet? They could wake up together like normal people. They could laugh and ride and argue over whose turn it was to do the dishes. And Grace would get over her hang-ups once Rachel wasn't around to strip her self-esteem.

Cassie's chest swelled with hope and even the birds chirped with fresh optimism.

She flung her arms around his neck, no longer caring about Santiago's return. Rachel would be out of their life. Out of Grace's life. It didn't matter what Santiago reported because Alex was going to have sole custody. And he was a wonderful father and Grace would be better off with just her dad anyway.

But then cold reason snapped her back to reality.

"Rachel will never give up her rights," she said slowly. "Grace is how she controls you."

"I know," Alex said. "But that's stopping now. It's not fair to Grace. And it's not fair to you."

She blinked, still finding it hard to believe. He was finally going to pay off Rachel? The woman would be gone? "So we won't have to meet on a plane somewhere?" she asked, her voice shaky. "Because I have to admit, I was considering it."

He skimmed a tender finger over her cheek. "That won't be necessary."

"What did you offer? Lots of money?"

"Half of everything," he said. "And the estate," he added, as though an afterthought. But there was a tiny moment when his eyes flickered, and she saw the regret he was working hard to conceal.

She jerked backwards. "Your home! But you can't do that! You love it there. Won't she take money?"

"I've already tried. Many times. And she knows what I treasure most. So she can have it. Maybe now she'll finally be happy."

Cassie just stared, struggling to absorb the enormity of what he was giving up. Her throat felt thick and a coldness clamped around her chest. His features blurred and she realized she was crying.

"You can't do that." She pressed her wet face into his shirt. "It's not right."

"It's the only way," he said. "She's getting worse. More manipulative. Grace is always worrying about her mother's reaction, the body image issues. Rachel lacks a normal mother's feelings."

So Gramps had been right. Grace did fear her mother. But Alex already suspected that. She should have realized he understood the situation. And had already analyzed it to pieces. Still...to give up his family estate.

"Where will we live?" she asked, raising her head. "Where could you possibly be happy after that?"

"Wherever you are," he said. "Some place with a good school where Grace can finally make friends. But away from here. Maybe Kentucky. We'll be fine."

However, the muscles in his shoulders bunched and she realized it wouldn't be as easy as he made it sound. Of course, he'd want to move away. He wouldn't want to drive by the Sutherland Estate every day and see Rachel ensconced in his ancestral home. That would only make him bitter. Maybe he'd turn bitter anyway. Maybe he'd regret such an enormous sacrifice.

"If Grace is happy and you're happy," he added quickly, as if reading her mind, "I will be too."

She studied him, silent for a moment. He did look younger, more carefree, the sparkle in his blue eyes almost brilliant. And maybe he would be happy. It would be easier for her. She'd already moved away before and done okay, even though she'd been aching for Alex. But this time she'd be with him. And Grace.

But not Gramps. He'd be all alone. In striking range of a very rich and vindictive woman.

"What about Gramps?" She glanced over her shoulder toward the thin figure waiting by the path. "Will he be all right? Living this close to Rachel?"

Alex gave an emphatic shake of his head. "No. We'll have to persuade him to move with us."

Her breath escaped in a relieved sigh. She should have known Alex wouldn't desert her grandfather to face Rachel's wrath alone. "I don't mind being poor," she said, rising on her toes and wrapping her arms back around his neck. "I can get a new job, maybe teach riding lessons, train a few horses. We'll get by."

He chuckled and she could feel his mouth smiling against her hair. "If you want to, sweetheart," he said. "But we won't be that poor. Just not as rich. In fact, we should buy your grandfather's horses. Maybe look for a club where we can play polo."

She gave a delighted nod. It was wonderful he'd consider picking up a mallet again. He was too good a player to walk away from a sport he'd enjoyed. And no wonder he wasn't worried about Santiago trashing the college sale. Gramps no longer needed a buyer. In fact, her grandfather would be able to relax and ride for fun. They'd all live together as a family and he could work as much or as little as he wanted. It was all so unbelievably wonderful, she felt almost weightless with joy.

"We should celebrate," Alex said. "Go out for dinner. Just the two of us. Or maybe go up in the plane." His hand cupped her bottom. "Fly somewhere, like Kentucky."

"To look at properties?" she asked.

"Exactly," he said. But he gave a mischievous grin and

when he tugged her between his hips, it was obvious he was thinking of far more pleasurable things. And quite honestly, that was fine with her.

CHAPTER THIRTY

The plane dipped a silver wing then smoothly, almost imperceptibly, banked toward the left. Cassie pressed closer to the window, peering down at the acreage below. They'd already flown over four lovely properties, none of them a fraction the size of the immense Sutherland Estate but still attractive homes.

This particular property was every bit as impressive as the others and the barn had a brick courtyard with adjoining paddocks. The grass looked lush and inviting, and best of all a sparkling ribbon of blue separated two adjoining fields. Grace would love riding Freckles across the brook, and numerous trails crisscrossed acres of leafy forest.

"The brook is the boundary," Alex said. "And the adjoining field and forest aren't for sale. Definitely unsuitable. Just like the rest we saw today."

She straightened in her seat. His agent had sent coordinates for ten properties, all in Kentucky, but so far Alex hadn't been very enthused. Of course, his expectations were way higher than hers.

He kept checking his watch and using the intercom to converse with the pilot. Obviously nothing would ever match his estate but his lack of enthusiasm left a sinking feeling in her stomach.

"Having second thoughts?" she asked.

"Not at all." He gave a reassuring smile. "But I want to get back to Grace."

"You worry about her being with Rachel? Even for an hour or two?"

"Santiago is there until eight," Alex said. "As long as I'm home by then everything will be okay."

He hadn't really answered her question but the grim line of his mouth revealed his concern. It was probably fortunate that Freckles wasn't stabled at the Sutherland barn yet, although it was bizarre to have to worry about a horse that belonged to Rachel's daughter.

But Cassie and Alex had found Freckles together. Had gone off on a private plane ride, just like now. And clearly Rachel was a strong believer in retaliation.

Cassie rubbed her hands over her arms.

"Cold?" Alex draped his arm over her shoulders. "We can adjust the heat."

"No, it's fine." But it was impossible to block her darker thoughts. Gramps was home alone with the horses, and he had mentioned some untimely events. And Rachel had stabbed Alex once. Long ago, but still…

"Rachel wouldn't drive over to Gramps' house again, would she?" Cassie asked, tilting her head. "Has she received your offer yet?"

Alex was silent for so long she thought he might not answer.

"I'm not sure," he finally said. "But if she's given the estate as well as assets, she should be content. She always wanted the property. And if she feels like she's won, there'd be no reason for her to hurt your horses…or anyone else."

"What?" Cassie's heart slammed against her ribs. "You've considered that possibility? About her hurting Gramps, or me?"

"I have thought about it," Alex said bleakly. "That's why I have safeguards in place."

"But that's not why you're giving up your home, is it?" she asked.

"No," he said. "I'm doing what's best for Grace."

Cassie pressed her fingers together. Nine years ago he'd given up their relationship for his daughter so it wasn't completely shocking he'd walk away from the home he loved. And it was admirable he'd sacrifice everything now, except sometimes she felt like an extra in a movie. And that he was always willing to send her away based on his beliefs about Grace.

"It's okay," Alex said, squeezing her shoulder. "We'll find a new home. One that's safe from Rachel. And I'm not going to talk about her, or complain. She's still the mother of my child. Just know that I'll take care of the situation."

Like he took care of everything else, she thought, with a shade of sadness. Whatever was best for him. And Grace. She stared down at her hands, stiffly folded on her lap. "I know you took care of finding that job for me," she said. "The one at the Center. When we were checking out Freckles, I couldn't understand how Wally knew Grace's age."

"That wasn't really a secret. You said you never wanted to see me again. I just made it easier." His voice was level but the hand on her shoulder tightened and she could feel his tension.

"I didn't know though," she said slowly. "Gramps let it

slip this morning."

"What does it matter?"

She stared down at her clasped fingers, not quite sure why it bothered her. All her life, Alex had handled things. He had the money and the power, along with an ingrained belief that he should always do his duty. He fiercely protected his own, and once he made a decision it was a done deal. And usually that had been a good thing, working in her favor…until it hadn't.

"What if I hadn't wanted to leave?" she asked. "What if it would have been better for me to stay and help Gramps? Would you have arranged for a more tempting offer?"

He shrugged, but it wasn't a gesture of confusion. He knew exactly what he'd have done. She eyed him, letting him know she wanted an answer. Knowing he wouldn't lie.

"It was better if you moved away," he said. "Easier. So, yes, there would have been a better offer."

"Easier for who?"

"Easier for Rachel," he said. "And therefore better for Grace."

"Darn, I should have held out for a bigger offer." She tried to sound flippant but it was hard to hide her sense of betrayal. Which was ridiculous because of course he'd always choose what was best for Grace. She knew that. He'd never pretended otherwise.

But now it was Rachel who was receiving an offer. Rachel who no longer fit into Grace's life. However, there was no way for Cassie to ever get back those lost years with her grandfather. No way to completely forget how desperately she'd longed to move home.

She stared down at her clenched hands, trying to shake off her resentment. She could have come home any time and visited. For a while, her grandfather had even offered to pay the travel costs. She was the one who always found reasons to stay away. That couldn't be blamed on Alex.

But Cassie's emotions were bubbling now, spurred by a growing sense of insecurity and the knowledge that she'd never be first in his life. And if Grace didn't want her around, what would he do then?

Alex though, seemed to think everything was perfect. Already his hands were moving back over her shoulders, his mouth skimming over her throat, a tease of fingers and lips that sent heat zapping to her core. Interesting that he could arouse her so quickly when she really wasn't in the mood for sex. What she needed was reassurance.

"Didn't you ever want to call me?" she asked, her voice cracking. "Didn't you wonder how I was doing? Especially in the beginning."

He stilled as if realizing she was still upset, then pressed his mouth against her ear. "Every day," he whispered. "But your grandfather made me promise not to."

Cassie winced. She remembered Gramps saying he'd told Alex to stay away. Hadn't realized that included her as well. And Alex took his promises seriously. One thing his parents had drilled into him was that a Sutherland never shirked their duty.

"But how could you just…stop thinking about me?"

"I couldn't," he said, cradling her face now, his eyes boring into hers. "And every Monday, your activity reports would arrive and I despised myself for reading them. And every month I'd send your grandfather plane vouchers and pray you'd come home. Yet pray you wouldn't. When you landed that job in California, I knew you had moved on. And it didn't seem right to watch over you anymore."

"Wait." She jerked backwards. "You had reports? From Wally?"

"No, the Sutherland team of investigators."

She still gripped her fingers, not sure if she was annoyed or comforted or simply shocked that he dealt with investigators. He spoke about them casually too, as if he used them on a regular basis.

"The reports were confidential," he added. "Wally never knew the extent of my interest. That promotion you received was fairly earned." He reached for her hands. "I just needed to make sure you were okay. Without breaking my word to your grandfather. Please forgive me?"

She thought about it for a moment then gave a little nod. "I find it strange that you have investigators though. Guess I don't know much about Sutherland Holdings."

"We invest in a broad range of equity securities. We don't actively manage anything. But we always need strategic intelligence."

"They weren't peeking in my windows or anything, were they?"

"God, no. Nothing like that."

"But where were they?" She tilted her head, curious now. She couldn't remember ever having the sense that someone was watching. "The grounds are monitored. Strangers can't just wander around. So how did they know what I was doing?"

"Well," he said, tracing the underside of her wrist with

his thumb. "It was so long ago I barely remember. And I was busy with a takeover at the time so details are foggy."

She gave a disappointed nod. It was a long time ago and he *was* a busy man.

"But I remember on July 4," he went on, "there was only a skeleton staff working at the Center. And you were holding a horse for a farrier and he noticed your boots were getting worn."

"And a few days later," she said thoughtfully, "Ariat sent us a shipment of boots." Everyone had been ecstatic when the company had sent boxes of boots to the Center. For advertising purposes, they'd claimed. And there had been eight pairs exactly her size.

"And the week before Father's Day," he went on, "you were hitchhiking to town on your day off because you wanted to find a gift for your grandfather."

Cassie gave a little nod. It had started to rain, a cold damp wetness, and she'd been so depressed thinking of Gramps and Alex and his new baby. But a woman in a Ford truck had picked her up and they'd ended up going for an impromptu lunch and having a delightful time. And she'd figured she must have a guardian angel somewhere.

And there were other details and other incidents and clearly they were etched in Alex's mind, but she didn't need to hear any more. He'd always looked out for her, always would. And she tapped down the little voice that warned she'd never be more than second on his list. Because as long as he never had to decide between her and Grace, that didn't even matter.

And she arched up in the seat, pressed her mouth against his and fervently kissed him, wishing they hadn't lost so much time over the years.

She heard his hiss of pleasure. Then he tilted her sideways, taking control, his mouth turning her dizzy with desire. And by the time he scooped her up and carried her to the bed, her only thought was the hope that he had made a long enough flight plan.

CHAPTER THIRTY-ONE

The sun poked over the horizon, bright, warm and full of promise. Cassie topped up the horses' water buckets as they munched their morning hay. Freckles gave a friendly nicker, acting as if he'd lived in Gramps' barn his entire life. She gave him an extra pat, then coiled the water hose and headed back to the house.

He'd been the perfect find. Quiet enough to take Grace on a relaxing trail ride but also trained and dependable on the polo field. He might not be the fastest horse but he was definitely the type to instill confidence in a rider. The fearless kind that did his job, no matter the circumstances.

Today Alex even planned to join them in hitting some balls. Ginger's cuts had healed enough to carry a saddle, and she'd be a great mount for an advanced player. Cassie still found it unbelievable he'd quit playing. All their time apart she'd been picturing him with Rachel, working together and having fun with the horses.

She climbed the steps to the verandah, remembering his endearing grin after he gave the perfect pass. The affectionate way he'd tap her helmet at the end of a game, win or lose. He usually played position number two, preferring to set up teammates to score but he was also like a brick wall on defense. Lightening quick with his stick but rattling off impossible no-look passes that always left her inspired and a tiny bit envious.

His skills would be rusty now, of course, but they'd come back. And he'd always been a generous player, never needing the limelight and quick to welcome new players and spectators to the game. Maybe some day both Gramps and Grace would wear the Sutherland colors. Then they'd have four players, enough for an amateur team. It had always been Cassie's hope to participate in the Club's Family Day, instead of watching alone from the sidelines. But though Gramps liked to train, he wasn't much one for playing games. She couldn't imagine him racing after a ball if he thought it would be better for the horse to slow down and practice flexing.

She pushed open the screen door, still smiling at the thought of her grandfather. He stood by the kitchen counter, his gray hair rumpled from sleep.

"Good morning," she called gaily.

He nodded but didn't speak. She pulled off her boots, poured two cups of coffee and set them on the kitchen table. He still didn't say a word. By this point he'd usually grilled her about the horses: how each one looked, if their legs were cold and tight and if they'd cleaned up their feed. But he remained silent. In fact, his face looked oddly flushed.

Maybe he'd been lifting something. She glanced around in concern. But nothing looked out of place and he appeared to have just risen. "Did you sleep okay?" she asked.

"Yup," he said. But he shuffled his feet, head down and preoccupied with the counter top. He didn't ask about the horses, or who she was going to ride first or what time Grace was arriving. Didn't say a word about Santiago or

Rachel or Alex. It was almost as if he were embarrassed.

And then she realized. A flush of heat warmed her cheeks. After yesterday's plane trip, Alex had driven her home. They'd remained outside on the porch, talking about the Kentucky properties and even though he'd been in a hurry to get back to Grace, he'd lingered a moment. Actually several moments. Long, passionate moments. His tongue had been deep in her throat, his knowing hands all over her, and she remembered she'd been moaning…

She guessed her face was now as pink as her grandfather's.

She cleared her throat. "Alex and I are together again," she said quietly. "Guess you know that."

"Know it now," Gramps muttered.

She picked up her coffee mug and pressed it to her mouth. It was too hot to drink but it gave her something to do with her hands. At least he'd only heard them. All the major action had happened on the plane. But whenever she and Alex were close the air sparked. Even now she was breathing a little faster, although that could also be related to her discomfort.

She could feel Gramps' gaze. He was finally looking at her, not so embarrassed now. In fact, his expression was rather reproachful.

"He's not married, Gramps," she said, sighing and setting down her mug. "Hasn't been for years. And I've never stopped loving him."

"I figured that. But sneaking around, hiding a state away. That's no way to live. Not for my girl." His voice strengthened. "You deserve more."

She pulled in a careful breath and leaned back in the chair. So he'd overheard her and Alex talking. But obviously he hadn't heard the full story.

"Alex is moving with me," she said. "And we're not certain if it will be Kentucky. So far he hasn't seen any properties he likes."

"He's moving?" Gramps gave an incredulous snort. "I don't believe it. He'll never leave Grace."

"But he's not leaving her. She's coming too."

"Rachel will never let that happen." Her grandfather rubbed a hand through his hair, messing it even more. "That kid is her golden ticket. The reason she can live on the estate. And a social climber like her is never happy unless she's lording it over everyone."

"Yes, Alex knows that. That's why he's giving Rachel the estate."

Gramps' eyes widened. He flattened his scarred hands over the table and slowly dropped into a chair. "But Alex can't give up his home. His father would roll over in the grave. That was the only thing Alex's parents cared about, even more than that big Thoroughbred stud. That horse was really something..."

He paused, as if puzzled that anyone would care more about land than a horse.

"But he is giving it up," she said. "And Alex and I both want you to move with us."

Her grandfather just stared across the table. He didn't look comforted. If anything, he looked wary.

"Don't you want to live with us?" She tilted her head, dismayed by his reaction.

"I don't know," he said. "I like it here. My house, my bed, my barn."

"Don't worry," she said. "There will be lots of space. And Grace just found Freckles. She'll want a place that's good for horses."

Her grandfather gave a reluctant smile. "I'm sure any place Alex buys will have top notch horse facilities. But I really don't see this working out." He sobered. "After all this time, I assumed you were over him. And I don't want you to get hurt. Not again."

"This time is different." She folded her arms, rather hurt by his lack of enthusiasm. "Alex already met with his lawyers. He's quite prepared to walk away."

"It's not that," Gramps said. "We both know once he makes up his mind, there's no changing it. But right now Rachel has everything she wants. The land, the money, the man. She won't give it up."

"But she doesn't have Alex. They barely talk."

Gramps waved a dismissive hand. "She doesn't have his love. But she can still trot him out to social functions by using Grace's presence. So she has the status that he brings. And that's what she really wants." His expression darkened. "I bet she'd rather him dead than give him up to you."

"Gramps!" Cassie jerked forward, then pressed back against the chair, struggling to stay calm. She never raised her voice to her grandfather. But the thought of something happening to Alex was too horrible to contemplate. And she couldn't forget that white scar on his lower ribs.

"I'm just pointing out that Grace would be a rich little girl," Gramps said. "And Rachel is her mother. It'd be the perfect solution."

"Rachel can't do anything," she heard herself saying while at the same time her mind whirled. Alex was bigger, stronger, smarter. And extremely wary. Rachel would never get close to him with a knife again, and it was doubtful the woman knew enough about cars or planes to resort to sabotage. Though it might be possible to sneak some poison into the poolhouse. But then Rachel would be putting Grace at risk as well. And most likely she'd be caught and a lengthy prison sentence wouldn't do much to enhance her precious status.

"She can't hurt Alex," Cassie repeated, more firmly now. "He knows her too well."

"Maybe," Gramps said, his voice solemn. "But once she learns his intentions, I bet she'll feel like hurting someone."

CHAPTER THIRTY-TWO

"When are we going to Cassie's, Dad?" Grace asked. She scooped up a scampering kitten, giggling as it tried to escape. "It's almost eight o'clock and I don't want to be late."

"I need to talk to your mother first," Alex said. He paced back to the front of the barn and checked the ring. Several horses were trotting circles, kicking up tiny plumes of dust, but none of the riders were Rachel. And there were no horses in the field or on the gallop track.

"Mom's not here," Grace said, her words muffled by the kiss she was planting on the kitten's nose. "She and Santiago went somewhere."

"In a car or on a horse?"

"In a car." Grace placed the kitten back in the stall and carefully bolted the door.

Alex nodded, resisting the urge to ask Grace about her mother's mood. It was unusual for Rachel to leave the barn so early but she'd probably received his offer. No doubt she'd charged into town to meet with her lawyers. He wished he'd seen her first though, so he could gauge her reaction. She'd either be ecstatic…or bitter.

"Did your mother have her riding clothes on?" he asked, deciding that was a permissible question. And not one that would unfairly test Grace's loyalties.

"I don't remember," Grace said. "She and Santiago were in the office. She doesn't like me bothering her there."

Rachel didn't like Grace bothering her anywhere, Alex thought. And that only reaffirmed that he'd made the right decision.

"Wait one moment." He turned and strode back down the aisle and around the corner to the office.

Two coffee cups sat on the desk. He picked up the cup with red lipstick on the rim. Only half finished and still lukewarm. Obviously Rachel had left in a hurry. Maybe eager to sign the deal?

He pulled out his phone and called his lawyer. "Any news yet?"

"No. But we couriered the document. Haven't heard anything so there's still time to withdraw. It's really far too generous—"

"Let me know as soon as you hear anything," Alex said. He palmed his phone. Yesterday he'd been positive Rachel would leap at the offer, but today he wasn't so certain. If she didn't go for this, he had nothing left to give. He'd never imagined a day when he'd even consider walking away from his ancestral home but he could almost feel the shackles lifting. And he wanted it finalized.

However, his sense of unease was growing, and it was a feeling he'd learned never to ignore. Especially when dealing with a conscienceless person like Rachel. He wished she'd come after him but Grace was an easier target. And they both knew their child was his biggest vulnerability.

He strode back to Grace. "Do you have a favorite horse

here?" he asked, keeping his voice casual.

"They're all my favorites," she said, wrinkling her nose at the absurdity of his question. "You know that."

"But have you bandaged or brushed one lately?"

"Just Ginger for the last month. And my special medicine really worked. Cassie said she can be ridden with a saddle again."

"That's great," Alex said, the tightness in his shoulders easing. Both Ginger and Freckles were safe at Cassie's. So that left only the kittens. "I wonder if your new horse likes cats," he said. "Want to find out?"

"Definitely!"

Just as he hoped, Grace grabbed the idea with gusto.

"We should take over a kitten today," she added. "Cassie said her grandfather's old cat died this spring. And he really likes cats, almost as much as horses. Maybe he'll even want one."

"So you're saying we should take over all the kittens?"

Grace's eyes widened. This was clearly going better than she expected. "Yes, we should take all of them. And Smokey too, of course." She bounced up and down in the aisle. "I'll get their cage. You get their food. This will be so much fun."

She bolted toward the tack room, talking excitedly about how she wanted to put a kitten on Freckles' back. Alex didn't much care where she put them, as long as the kittens were safe. And out of Rachel's reach.

◆

"This old stud stall is the safest spot," Cassie said, staring in bemusement at the eight kittens scampering around

Grace's feet. "I just cleaned it. And the mesh wire goes all the way up so even the mom can't climb out."

"Great," Grace said. "But I'll sit with them for a minute and make sure they're not scared. You can hold Oreo. He'd be the perfect cat for your grandfather."

She plunked a black and white kitten into Cassie's hands then squeezed back into the stall and shut the door before any other kittens could escape. The little kitten in Cassie's arms blinked then closed his eyes, happy to curl against a warm chest and grab a nap.

"Looks like the car ride tired him out," Alex said, stroking the kitten's head with a gentle finger. "We had the roof down. Grace thought they'd like the fresh air." He leaned closer, his voice lowering. "Sorry, but I was afraid to leave them. I think Rachel is with her lawyers now. Hopefully she'll sign and this will be over."

Cassie traced the white in the middle of the kitten's face, her finger linking with Alex's. She wanted to ask all sorts of questions but not where Grace might hear. However, like Gramps, it was obvious Alex was wary of Rachel's reaction. And the fact that he feared for the safety of Grace's kittens was heartbreaking. And troubling.

"No problem," she said. "They can stay as long as necessary. Gramps has been talking about getting another cat."

"Thanks for your understanding. With all of this." Alex's voice was deep with meaning.

She shifted the kitten to her left arm, looped her finger tighter around his and tugged him down the aisle to the doorway. "You're worrying about everyone else," she whispered. "But what about you? Are you safe?"

He didn't pretend not to understand. "I'm going into

town now to assess Rachel's...thought process. But she won't ever be alone again with Grace. And I won't be alone with her either, not without lawyers present."

Cassie nodded but couldn't dismiss her grandfather's warnings. "And maybe you should be careful, you know, about what you eat."

His expression darkened but he gave a reluctant nod. "I've thought of that," he said. Then his head slanted, covering her lips in a reassuring kiss. And his awareness was comforting. He was a careful man and probably had always been wary of Rachel.

She stopped worrying as his kiss deepened. Soon they wouldn't have to hide from anyone. They'd be able to wake up together in the mornings and go to sleep together each night. And he didn't mind signing over the estate, and it was clear he loved her every bit as much as she loved him. Still, it was a huge sacrifice.

She pulled back from his embrace and studied his face, remembering how she'd ached for Gramps' little farm. That homesick feeling had never gone away. And this was so much bigger. "You're sure?" she asked. "About walking away from your home? Because we could work out something. I understand everything now—"

"It's the only way Grace will ever have a normal life," he said. "You love kids. And she already likes and trusts you."

Cassie made an agreeable sound, but it wasn't quite the answer she was looking for. Probably she'd always have insecurities, simply because of how ruthlessly Alex had once cut her out of his life. But this time was different. This time she was good for Grace.

Then his mouth was back over hers, as if sensing her

misgivings. And if the passion in his kiss was evidence of his love, he had plenty enough. He proved remarkably adept at holding her close, and yet keeping his chest tilted so he wouldn't squash the kitten.

He reluctantly raised his head. "I have to go now," he murmured. "And finish this. But I'll be back to join you and Grace. I threw my mallet in the car so we could hit some balls later. Hopefully, we'll be celebrating tonight."

He pressed one last kiss against her mouth then turned and strode to his car. She stepped out into the driveway, waved and watched long after the convertible disappeared down the road, rather comforted by the velvety soft kitten snoozing in her arms. By suppertime, this would be over. One way or another.

She walked back into the barn and carefully placed the kitten in the straw beside its mother. Three of the kittens were sleeping. The other four were exploring the bright straw, leaping and rolling in play. They were all adorable and she sat down on the straw and let them climb over her lap, enjoying their antics. She'd have to let Gramps know they were here so he could see them before they left.

If they ever left.

Everything depended on Rachel. Cassie couldn't imagine a mother giving up parental rights, not for any amount of land or money. But Alex was certain Rachel wanted the estate. Gramps, however, suspected Rachel really desired Alex. One of them was wrong.

She wiggled a piece of straw, smiling as a gray kitten rolled on its back, grabbing at the stalk with all four paws. It quickly tired, curled in a ball and fell asleep against her knee. She stroked his back with a light finger. They were so little, so helpless. And they were here because Alex feared Rachel might hurt them. That thought was sobering.

She rose to her feet and eased from the stall. It was important to think positive. Rachel would sign. Gramps would agree to move. And by this time tomorrow, Alex would be able to discuss the situation with Grace. She'd be able to help choose their new home. That would surely smooth the transition.

Cassie gave her head a shake. Calling it a transition was downplaying its enormity, and the extent of Alex's sacrifice. For her, for Grace. Her chest warmed and her heart beat double time. Grace might never know the depth of her father's love but Cassie certainly did.

And the least she could do was stop daydreaming and help Grace with her new horse. They'd need to find a thick pad for Freckles before any kittens were placed on his back. Even though they were small, their claws were sharp. And where the heck was Grace?

"Hey, Grace," she called, stepping outside the barn and glancing around.

But Grace wasn't anywhere in sight. In fact, Freckles' paddock was empty except for a half flake of hay, a bucket of water and his blue halter lying beside a polo mallet.

Cassie circled the rest of the paddocks. But she couldn't find Grace or Freckles. They weren't in the round pen, or behind the barn, or enjoying the sweet grass in front of the verandah.

Digger stared over the top rail of his paddock, eyeing the path that led to the brook. Had Grace already headed down to the water? That wasn't the plan. It wasn't even hot yet and they were planning to go to the field and hit some balls. And Grace shouldn't ride off alone, no matter how quiet her horse.

Cassie frowned then turned and strode to the house. "Hey, Gramps," she called, pushing open the screen door. "Did you see Grace this morning? Did she say where she was going?"

Her grandfather looked up from a dog-eared horse magazine. "Didn't see her," he said. "Did she walk off?"

"No, she rode off. On Freckles."

"What about her lesson?" Gramps asked. "She's not the type to ride away without permission. Was she upset about something?"

"No. She was really happy about bringing her cat and kittens, In fact, I was talking to Alex and didn't even realize she'd tacked up."

"Why did she bring her kittens?" her grandfather asked. "Alex knows I never liked it when students brought dogs. I suppose cats are cuter and don't bark… I see." He gave a glum sigh. "He must be worried about Rachel. And how she might react. That's a bad sign."

He abruptly slapped the magazine on the table and lurched to his feet. "You need to find that kid. Right now."

Cassie had already pulled out her phone, but looked up, startled by the whip in her grandfather's voice. "She's probably at the brook, Gramps. No need to worry."

She pressed Grace's number. But Grace didn't answer her phone or Cassie's text.

"She's not supposed to use her cell when she's riding," Cassie said, shoving her phone back in her pocket. "So I'll take Digger and ride down to the swimming hole. Call me if she shows up, okay?"

Gramps nodded but she didn't like the disapproving look in his face. "Find her fast," he said. "Alex didn't leave her here so she could go riding off alone, especially under these circumstances. And if Rachel would kill some kittens in order to get back at Alex, she's not very stable. She already knows the easiest way to hurt him is through Grace."

Cassie just stared, the blood draining from her face. Gramps was always so honest, so blunt. And he didn't even know that Rachel had once stuck a steak knife in Alex's ribs.

She wheeled, pushed open the screen door and raced toward Digger's paddock.

CHAPTER THIRTY-THREE

Digger's saddle and bridle were in the barn and Cassie didn't want to waste precious time tacking up. She snapped a lead rope on the horse's halter, then tied the other end to form a makeshift bridle, her grandfather's words replaying in her head, stoking her worst fears. She'd never forgive herself if Rachel hurt Grace.

She grabbed a piece of Digger's mane, hopped twice and swung onto his back. He sidled sideways, surprised by her urgency, but she straightened him out and seconds later they were charging toward the wooded path behind the barn.

She sat back, trying to slow him to a trot before they hit the trees. But he was excited now and simply pushed his nose against the halter. She grabbed his mane as he leaped over a fallen tree then pounded down the path, galloping like an enthusiastic steeplechaser. At this speed, they'd probably scare Freckles and Grace when they burst out by the brook, but there was no slowing Digger.

She ducked just in time to miss a low-hanging branch. Jerked backwards as he scrambled over a scatter of rocks. Minutes later, they burst into the clearing by the brook. Digger arched his neck and slowed to a bouncy trot, clearly proud of the swift trip and anticipating the chance to nibble some grass.

But the clearing was empty.

She pulled him in a tight circle, staring in dismay. The path ended here. There was no other place a horse could go. And Grace definitely wasn't around. Hadn't even been here. The grass was dewy fresh, unmarked by hooves.

"Dammit," she muttered, yanking out her phone and checking the screen.

No calls. No texts. And when she pressed Grace's number, the girl still didn't answer. She must have ridden in the opposite direction, to the south field. But that didn't make sense. Why hadn't she waited for Cassie? She hadn't even taken her polo mallet.

"Come on, boy," Cassie said, pulling Digger's head around and urging him back up the path. He seemed disappointed they were leaving the brook without a single bite of grass, but he galloped gamely, his stride slowing as he neared the barn.

She pushed him past the barn and paddocks, toward the house. Gramps was pacing back and forth on the verandah, his mouth a flat line.

"Did you see her?" she asked, trying to stop Digger. But his blood was pumping now and she could only wheel him in a circle.

"No," Gramps said. "But Santiago called. Didn't say much. Just that he's coming to pick up Grace."

"No way," Cassie said. "Alex wants her to stay with us."

"That's what I told him. But he was adamant that it was for the best."

"Maybe it's good that Grace is off riding." Cassie glanced down the empty driveway. "At least she's away from the barn. She's definitely not getting into Santiago's car."

"But Rachel is her mother," Gramps said. "If she's with Santiago, Grace will have to leave. Even Alex can't stop them."

Cassie wrapped her hand more tightly around the horse's mane, trying to steady her breathing. Struggling to think. Obviously Santiago would just deliver Grace to Rachel. And it was horrible to have to worry about Grace's safety around her mother, the very person who was expected to protect her the most. But it was something Alex had dealt with for nine years. No wonder he'd been ambivalent about Cassie's return. That type of fear was paralyzing, and overrode every other emotion.

She blew out a choked sigh. "The main thing is to keep her away from Santiago and Rachel," she said. "I'll take Grace into town and wait for Alex at the lawyer's office. Or maybe it's best to call Alex and ask him to come back. Then he can reassure her about the…situation."

Digger tossed his head and she turned him in another circle. Grace hadn't been told anything yet. And even though she liked Cassie, seeing her dad with another woman would be upsetting.

"Oh, no," she muttered, slumping so low her face touched Digger's mane. Now she realized why Grace had ridden away. She must have seen Alex's kiss. Grace had been playing with the kittens while they lingered outside the barn door. They'd been holding the black kitten. Whispering and kissing and thinking of the future.

Not thinking of Grace.

She straightened, her legs tightening around Digger's sides. "I think she saw Alex kiss me. She's probably upset and headed home. I'll try to catch her before she reaches the estate. Phone Alex," she called, turning Digger toward the field. "Let him know what's going on."

Digger was already cantering toward the field, picking up on her urgency. Or maybe he was just eager for the excuse to gallop on a path that had previously been reserved for sedate warming up and cooling down.

They careened into the woods. The trail was level and not as rough as the brook path, and Digger knew it well. Trees whipped past in a blur. She only had to duck once and then they broke from the forest and onto the south field where the cool shade changed to blinding sunlight. She shaded her eyes, glancing left and right, but the big field was empty.

Her worst fear was confirmed; Grace had headed home.

She urged Digger across the field, wind whipping her cheeks. She probably should have grabbed a saddle, but she'd galloped this route bareback plenty of times before. On far less dependable horses. However, she'd never felt such an insidious fear before and her hand was wrapped so tightly around Digger's mane it cut into her skin.

How long was Grace's head start? Fifteen, twenty minutes?

Even at Freckles' ambulatory speed, Grace might be close to the Sutherland Estate by now.

She chirped to Digger and his stride lengthened. "Good boy," she said, but the driving wind blew the words back in her face.

They crested another rolling field, his hooves pounding over the grass. There was still no sign of an upset little girl trotting home. There was no loose horse either so at least Grace hadn't fallen off. Although that might be a good thing. A fall would slow her down and keep her from riding into Santiago's and Rachel's clutches.

Digger's ground-covering gallop was rhythmic and rock steady now, his breathing even. Luckily he was very fit. Her own legs felt rubbery though, her seat not as secure. But pristine white rails glinted in the distance, and it was clear they were almost there.

The trail from the south side of the estate wove over a wooden horse bridge and then skirted the back of the gallop track. But it was a five-minute walk to the stables so there was still a chance to catch Grace before she rode into the open barn area. And possibly Santiago was still in his car. He definitely wouldn't pass Grace and Freckles on the horse path.

Luckily there was no way he and Rachel would be expecting to see Grace on a horse. Unless she'd called them on her cell. Which would be a normal reaction for an upset nine-year-old, even if she'd been warned not to use her phone while riding.

Cassie leaned further over Digger's neck, pushing him even faster, driven by fear and her rising guilt.

CHAPTER THIRTY-FOUR

Digger's stride was long and even, the steady drumming of his hooves reassuring. They rounded a stand of willow trees. His impulsion changed as his body coiled and his ears pricked. Cassie almost wept with relief.

Grace and Freckles trotted along the path, only thirty feet ahead. Grace was sitting tall in the saddle, her shoulders perfectly square. Despite Cassie's worry, she couldn't help but feel a burst of pride for the girl's improved riding skills.

Digger swept alongside Freckles who cocked a friendly ear but continued his obedient trot. Grace glanced sideways, her eyes widening in surprise. Then she scowled and jerked her head away.

"How was your ride?" Cassie asked, slowing Digger's trot to match Freckle's shorter steps. "You made good time."

Grace didn't speak. She just stared straight ahead, staring over Freckles' ears as if Cassie didn't exist.

"Did you canter in the field?" Cassie asked, talking over the drumming of the horses' hooves and the nervous pounding of her heart. *Ask questions. Try to get her talking.* "Did he buck at all?"

Grace's mouth remained clamped in a resentful line.

"Did he spook?" Cassie asked. "I bet he was afraid of the wooden bridge. That's really scary for horses. Even Digger was afraid. Any horse would be…"

"Freckles didn't spook," Grace said. "Not once. He didn't buck either."

"Even when you cantered?"

"We didn't just canter." Grace spoke grudgingly. "We galloped too. Well, it felt like a gallop."

"I think you probably did gallop," Cassie said. "Because Digger is very fast and we barely caught you. And Freckles is all sweaty, even on his flanks."

Grace twisted, checking the white lather on Freckles' flanks. She immediately pulled him to a walk. "Oh, no. Is he okay? I didn't want to hurt him. Did I ride him too hard?"

"He'll be fine," Cassie said quickly. "But maybe we should get off now and walk. Let both of the horses cool out a bit."

Grace halted Freckles and scrambled from the saddle. "I hope he's okay," she said. "I hope I didn't go too fast."

Cassie kept her expression solemn and dismounted beside Grace. Freckles was hot and sweaty, but not in any distress. However, Grace's concern for her horse was the easiest way to slow her down. And keep her talking.

"If you hold Digger," Cassie said, holding out the lead rope, "I'll check Freckles' respiration rate for you."

Grace automatically took the lead rope, and Cassie's worry eased another notch. The girl was obviously feeling betrayed, but at least she was no longer bolting for home. Cassie kept her gaze on Freckles' flank and her wrist watch, ostensibly measuring the horse's respiration.

"He's fine," she said after a minute. "But it's best to cool him out slowly. Maybe we should lead them back to Gramps' place."

"No! I'm not going back there." Grace's face was already flushed from heat and exertion, but now she whipped her head back and forth, her blotchy cheeks turning an angry red. "Freckles can live here from now on. And I don't want any more lessons from you."

Cassie's chest wrenched and she wished she and Alex had been more discreet. She placed the back of her hand over Freckles' chest, stalling for time, struggling to find the best words. However, she wasn't equipped for this. She was a horse trainer, not a psychologist. And no matter how much she cared for Grace, she wasn't a parent and it wasn't her place to tell Grace about her dad's plans.

Besides, if Grace resented Cassie so much, would Alex even want to move? He made no secret that his decisions were based on Grace's best interest. What if Grace insisted on living on the estate? Or worse, if Grace never wanted to see Cassie again?

"That's too bad," Cassie said gently. "Because I like giving you lessons. And I love riding with you. But we should check with your dad before you move Freckles home. It might be a few days before a stall is ready."

"No, there's an empty stall at the office end of the barn where Ginger used to be," Grace said. "I'll put Freckles there."

"But don't you need to check with your mom first? Or Santiago?" Cassie asked. "Just in case they need that stall for polo ponies?"

"Freckles *is* a polo pony," Grace said. "Besides, I'll tell Mom when he's in the stall. It's better than asking her first."

It sounded like Grace hadn't talked to Rachel and Santiago yet. They didn't even know Grace was close by. So there was no way they'd be watching the horse path. And the knowing glint in Grace's eyes when she spoke about asking permission after the fact reminded Cassie so much of Alex that she couldn't hold back a smile.

"That's a good idea about asking afterwards," Cassie said. "Once a horse is in a stall, they tend to keep it. Your dad did that with a few of my horses and your grandfather always let them stay."

Grace tilted her head, as if surprised by Cassie's agreement. She even gave a cautious nod. "Guess I'm a lot like Dad," she said.

Then her mutinous expression returned. "I saw you two kissing. But Dad won't move and leave me alone with Mom. I know he won't." However, the telltale quaver in her voice showed she wasn't completely certain.

"Of course he won't," Cassie said, resisting the impulse to reach out and give the confused girl a hug. "Your dad loves you more than anything in this world."

"So he won't leave me with Mom, right...?" Grace's beseeching eyes almost broke Cassie's resolve. She tightened her hands around Digger's lead line. The last thing Grace wanted were hugs from the woman she viewed as a potential home wrecker.

"I know he won't ever leave you," Cassie said. "Why don't you call and talk to him?"

"I can't." Grace kicked at the ground, her gaze fixed on the toe of her boot. "I called Mom and she was mad and yelling, and I dropped my phone in the field. That's when she said Dad was going to move away and leave me."

"Just a sec," Cassie said, trying her grandfather's number.

Gramps answered on the first ring. "Rachel refused to sign," he said without preamble. "Apparently she started screaming at her lawyer. Then stormed out in a huff. Did you find Grace?"

"Yes." Cassie pressed the phone closer to her ear, hoping Grace wouldn't hear Gramps' words. The girl was already terrified of her mother's moods. "We're on the horse path near the back of the Sutherland stables, on the side with all the paddocks."

"Okay. I'll tell Alex. He's busy with his lawyers now. Apparently Rachel and Santiago are still in town."

"Good." Cassie gave a relieved nod. "That makes it easier. But ask Alex to come here as soon as he's free. Grace needs to speak to him."

"Is she okay?" Gramps' voice softened. "The kid had quite a ride. Best to give the horses a break before coming back."

"We'll just stay on the path and wait for Alex," Cassie said. "And then figure it out. I might be riding Digger home alone."

"What about Freckles?"

"We can talk about that later," Cassie said. "I have to go."

"Sounds like there's a lot to work out," Gramps said. "It can't be easy dealing with a psychotic ex-wife."

Cassie turned her body slightly, conscious of Grace's rapt attention. She wished her grandfather wouldn't speak quite so loudly. "Yes," she said. "See you later."

"Did you tell him I galloped?" Grace asked as Cassie pocketed her phone. "And that Freckles didn't spook at anything?"

"You can tell him yourself," Cassie said, pulling at

Digger's lead line. Both horses were stretching their necks now, taking advantage of the break, and trying to snatch grass from the side of the path. "He'd like to hear that from you in person."

"Maybe I'll visit him sometime," Grace said. She tugged at her lower lip, oblivious to the fact that Freckles was standing on one of his reins. "You're not mad at me?"

"Just worried," Cassie said, lifting Freckle's leg and freeing the rein. *Worried about a lot of things. Like what Alex would do now that she and Grace weren't quite so cozy.* "I'll really miss you. Gramps will too."

"But you'll see me again. I have to pick up Smokey and the kittens."

Grace's statement hit like a splash of cold water, reminding Cassie exactly why the kittens had been stowed at her grandfather's barn. And it was premature to worry about her relationship with Grace when Rachel was still a threat.

She glanced down the horse path. The open paddock area at the back of the stable was only fifty feet away. It would be safer to take Grace and Freckles back to her grandfather's, just in case Rachel and Santiago arrived before Alex.

"I'm starving," Cassie said brightly. "Let's ride back to Gramps and order a pizza. A really big one. Then after lunch you can eat hit some balls with your dad...and you won't have to wait to take the kittens home."

"No," Grace said. "Freckles is tired. I'm going to put him in a stall so he can relax and eat some hay."

Cassie rubbed a hand over her forehead. After making a big deal about how tired and sweaty Freckles was, it was hard to argue that he should be ridden back to her grandfather's. But hopefully she could keep Grace here on the horse path, out of sight of anyone arriving in a car.

"Digger's tired too," Cassie said, feeling her horse's sweaty chest. "So I'll just walk around the path with you until your dad comes. It's shaded and there's a nice breeze. The horses can even eat grass."

Grace shook her head. "No, it's okay for Digger because he only has a halter. But Freckles has a bridle and it's harder to chew with a bit in his mouth. I'm going to lead him back to the barn now." She tugged at his reins then paused.

"If you're really hungry," she said slowly, "we can find a shaded paddock for Digger. He can stay there while you eat lunch with me in the barn. There's always fruit and sandwiches there."

Cassie blinked, the backs of her eyes pricking at the girl's generosity of spirit. Everything would be all right. Obviously Grace had a forgiving heart and was far more concerned about being ripped away from her father than seeing him kiss Cassie.

And there was no way she was turning down Grace's kind lunch offer. Or abandoning her to wait at the barn alone. If it wasn't safe to leave kittens around Rachel, it certainly wasn't safe to leave Freckles. Or Alex's sweet daughter.

"I'd love to have lunch with you," Cassie said, her voice so husky she had to clear it with a cough. "That's really thoughtful, considering everything. And I'm really glad, you know…" But her voice broke and all she could manage was a wobbly smile.

But this time Grace smiled back.

CHAPTER THIRTY-FIVE

The Sutherland stable still provided the delicious staff luncheons that Cassie remembered. By the time she and Grace untacked and cooled out their horses, the grooms had all drifted away. But though the lunch room was deserted there was still plenty of food.

"This is better than pizza," Cassie said. She took a last bite of her vegetable wrap and wiped her mouth with an elegant polo-themed napkin. "Thank you, Grace."

Grace gave an agreeable nod. "It's healthier," she said. "But pizza tastes better. And I like eating on your grandfather's verandah. Maybe tonight we can order pizza?" She kept her gaze locked on the fruit bowl, as if selecting an apple was a matter of great importance. "And I was hoping that maybe you could still give me lessons?" she added, keeping her gaze averted.

"Of course," Cassie said. "I like teaching you. But Santiago is the instructor here."

"Oh, I know you couldn't come here," Grace said quickly. "Anyway, it's probably best if Freckles goes back to your place. It's way better for him."

Way better. Even though they were sitting in buttery leather chairs in an air-conditioned viewing room stocked with unlimited food and a range of munchies that would delight any kid. Not to mention the beautiful oak stall with brass fixtures and top quality hay where Freckles now resided. It was sad Grace couldn't enjoy this beautiful estate. Even more tragic that she seemed to understand why. On the other hand, it meant she might not be too resistant to moving away.

"Freckles is always welcome at Gramps," Cassie said. "Or any place that we live. But you can talk to your dad about that. He'll help you figure out what's best."

"Okay," Grace said, comfortable again. She rose from the chair, waving a shiny red apple. "Maybe I'll even ride back with you this afternoon. But I'm going to take this apple to Freckles now. He deserves a treat for being so good. And I want to make sure he has enough hay."

Cassie nodded and accompanied her down the wide aisle and around the corner to Freckles' stall. She had no doubt the horse had plenty to eat. Grace had loaded up his stall with alfalfa, looking after his every need before going for her own lunch. If Grace did decide to ride back to Gramps' barn at least Freckles had enjoyed a few hours of pampering.

They slid open the stall door. Freckles gave a welcoming nicker, then shoved his nose back into his mound of hay. If he was embarrassed by the zebra-striped cooler Grace had covered him with, he didn't show it. He also didn't seem perturbed about being in a different barn, his third home in five days. There was nothing easier than a horse accustomed to the frenetic hustle of movie making.

"I love this horse." Grace wrapped her arms around Freckles' neck and gave him an enthusiastic hug. "He didn't buck or shy or do anything bad." She glanced over her shoulder at Cassie, her face solemn. "And I can't wait to hit polo balls on him with Dad…and you."

Cassie's breath caught in a moment of sheer relief. She didn't like hanging around the Sutherland barn, worrying that Santiago might arrive, demanding to take Grace to Rachel. But Grace was really opening up. The time spent together today had been invaluable.

"I can't wait either," Cassie said. And this time she didn't stop herself. She leaned forward and wrapped her arms around Grace in an impulsive hug.

Grace didn't pull away. She kept an arm around Freckles' neck, but put her other arm around Cassie and began talking about how some day she might even play at the Polo Club. So other kids could see how wonderful Freckles was and maybe realize they didn't need a fancy pony to have fun.

Cassie nodded, smiling along with Grace. The solitary ride across the fields had clearly cemented Grace's trust in Freckles. And boosted the girl's confidence. Having a good horse was like having a best friend, one that was always available. Freckles would certainly make Grace's out-of-state move less difficult.

That is, if Alex still wanted to move.

Cassie dropped her arms and stepped back. Gramps said Rachel had turned down the estate so there was no way Alex could move now. He wouldn't put Grace in front of a judge. Besides, Grace would never say anything negative about her mom. The girl wouldn't even admit that she feared her. So once again it was a deadlock.

"I think I should ride Freckles back today," Grace said, still smiling. "I just want him to be safe. Do you think he's rested enough?"

Cassie stared down at Grace's trusting face. They'd been so close to finding a solution, but Cassie's presence would always be a liability. And Rachel's trigger.

"Do you think he's rested up enough?" Grace repeated.

Cassie glanced at Freckles. The horse had already shoved his nose back in the hay. He didn't look tired, just relieved the hugging had stopped so he could continue eating.

"I think you're more tired than he is," Cassie said, struggling to keep her voice light. "But let's check with your dad."

She took a bracing breath and reached for her phone. Her hand froze over her pocket, struck by the significance of Grace's words. She'd just admitted she wanted Freckles safe. That must mean she didn't trust her mom. Even though she refused to verbalize that fear to Alex.

From outside a car door slammed.

"That must be your dad now," Cassie said, swinging around with renewed hope. Grace was finally opening up about her fears. She just needed to talk freely to her dad. And then maybe to a judge. But it wasn't Alex's voice they heard at the far end of the barn. It was Santiago.

"You're not going anywhere with him," Cassie said, placing a protective hand on Grace's shoulder. "Even if he says he has your mom's permission. You're staying here and waiting for your dad. Okay?"

Grace gave an emphatic nod. "I'm not leaving Freckles alone here," she whispered. "Just in case Mom is still in a bad mood."

Cassie blinked. She hadn't realized Grace had talked to her mother before she dropped her phone in the field. "Did you tell your mom or Santiago you were riding over here today?" she asked, keeping the concern from her voice.

"I tried to tell her," Grace said. "But Mom was yelling too much. She said I was going to live with her forever. And that it was all my fault Dad wanted to move away." Her lower lip quivered and her throat gave a convulsive swallow. "And she said a bad girl like me doesn't deserve to have any pets. So it's good Smokey and the kittens aren't here. Because she never likes anything Dad and I like."

Her words turned shrill and Cassie pressed a warning finger over her mouth. It was great Grace was finally acknowledging her real feelings, and hopefully she'd repeat them to Alex. But it was best if they remained quiet. There was no reason they'd be found in this back stall. Santiago didn't even know they were here.

"It sounds like he's talking to a groom," Cassie whispered, her tension easing. Santiago wouldn't dare muscle Grace in the car with both Cassie and a groom around, even if he had Rachel's permission.

"No," Grace said. "The grooms are gone. They don't come back until five o'clock."

Cassie swallowed. "Let's be really quiet then." She checked that her ring tone was muted and sent a hasty text to Alex: *Grace and I are at your barn. Santiago just arrived. Can you hurry?*

And then a second car door slammed and Cassie almost dropped her phone in the straw. Because there was no mistaking the second voice. Rachel had arrived, and judging from the sound she was clearly in a rage.

CHAPTER THIRTY-SIX

Grace edged sideways, pressing closer to Freckles. Santiago and Rachel were still talking outside the barn, and even though their words weren't discernible, it was clear they were arguing.

"She's really mad," Grace whispered. "And she won't like it that I lost my phone, and then she'll yell at me even more. She won't be happy about Freckles either. Especially since he came from your barn." Her eyes looked big in her pale face. "I better get him out of here."

"Wait." Cassie placed a cautionary hand on the door, slowing Grace's exit. The grooms were gone. If Rachel heard a stall door open and the sound of a horse's clopping feet, she'd rush down the aisle and investigate. But with any luck, she might not even notice Freckles. Or Cassie.

She winced, hating to imagine Rachel's reaction if she found Cassie inside the barn.

"I think we should climb over the stall door and tiptoe out the back," Cassie said. "We'll wait for your dad on the path, behind the back paddock where we put Digger."

"No," Grace said, her mouth flattening in a stubborn line. "I'm not leaving Freckles. Not when Mom's so mad. She never likes my pets. And it's the rider's responsibility to look after her horse."

"Or the instructor's," Cassie said. "How about if I stay here and look after Freckles? You can go to the poolhouse and wait. But be very quiet, okay. And don't come back to the stable until your dad gets you."

Grace thought for a moment then gave a little nod. "You'll take good care of Freckles? Promise you won't leave him alone with Mom?"

"I promise," Cassie said. "Now go."

She cupped Grace's leg and boosted her over the top of the door. It was no different than legging her onto a horse and Grace landed easily on the other side of the stall. But she lingered, obviously torn.

"Go on." Cassie gestured at the end door. "I'll take care of Freckles. And I'll see you soon."

"Thanks," Grace said. "And I'm really sorry for saying I didn't want lessons anymore. You're the best instructor ever. And please don't tell Mom I lost my phone. Not until Dad comes. He's the only one who can make her calm."

"I won't say anything," Cassie said, shooting an urgent look down the aisle. "But you go now."

She waited until Grace scampered out the back door, then turned and pulled off Freckles' cotton cooler. This stall was supposed to be empty. No reason to attract attention with a colorful blanket. She just hoped Rachel and Santiago stayed at the other end of the barn.

She sat down in the straw and sent Alex a second message. *Rachel and Santiago are both at the barn now. Text me back. Don't call.*

A rather cryptic message but he'd understand.

She propped her back against the wooden wall, cradling the phone on her lap. Freckles chewed his hay, unperturbed by a silent woman hiding in his stall. Or the angry voices outside.

Her phone vibrated and she snatched at it like a lifeline.
Where are you? Alex texted.
In the back stall with Freckles. Where are you?
Only 15 minutes away. But Rachel is upset. It's best if she doesn't see you.
I know, Cassie wrote. *So come quick.*
I will. Is Grace okay?
Yes, Cassie typed. *She's waiting for you in the poolhouse.*
She won't answer her phone. Is she okay?
She's anxious to see you, Cassie wrote. *But she dropped her phone in the field.*

She clutched her own cell as the voices moved closer, and try as she might, resentment mingled with her fear. She was the one hiding in the straw, protecting Freckles. But Alex wasn't concerned about her. He'd never made any secret that his life was focused on Grace. She knew and understood that. But right now, when her back was against the wall, sweating with fear, she needed to know that he was hurrying.

She stared at the screen, willing his next text to arrive. Contact with him made her feel less isolated. And several minutes had already passed. He should be here soon.

But when his next message arrived she could only stare: *I'll stop at the poolhouse on the way. Santiago will help you.*

She studied his words in disbelief. Sure, Santiago wasn't as erratic as Rachel but she didn't trust him either, despite Alex's assurances. The man did whatever Rachel asked. It was entirely possible they'd push Cassie beneath Freckles' feet and then swear that she was trampled. Which was quite absurd since Freckles was incapable of trampling anyone.

She shot a reassuring look at the placid horse. His nose

was still tucked in the hay, blithely unaware he was in a hostile barn. No doubt he was accustomed to a range of voices on a movie set, voices that were excited and loud and threatening.

Threatening?

She rose to a crouch, straining to hear. It was mainly Rachel talking. And her voice was definitely louder, more menacing. They were inside the barn now and Santiago was no longer saying much. It was all Rachel.

"Did you think I wouldn't find out?" Rachel was yelling. "That all this time you were working for Alex?"

"I was working for the family, for Grace, that's all—"

"Shut up! You betrayed me!"

"For God's sake, Rachel, put down the gun. Alex is coming. And if you anger him anymore he won't be so generous. He'll cut you off from everything."

"He can't cut me off from Grace. I'm her mother."

"But you're waving a gun. Clearly that makes you unstable. Any judge would agree…" Santiago's voice drifted. Cassie didn't know if the frightened pounding of her heart made his words harder to hear or if his voice had lowered. But she could only catch portions of his sentences now. And it was no wonder he sounded different. Almost desperate.

Rachel had a gun.

CHAPTER THIRTY-SEVEN

Cassie jerked up, crouched, then rose again, fear making it impossible to stay still. She was tempted to scramble over the top of the stall and bolt out the back door but the voices were too close. She could even see flashes of movement now: a shoulder, an arm, gleaming blond hair. Rachel seemed to be circling Santiago, her steps jerky.

"Just take the offer," Santiago was saying. "You'll have money as well as the estate. And you know you don't care about Grace. Alex does."

"And see him and our child with another woman!" Rachel spat. "That's never going to happen. I'd rather them both dead."

Cassie gasped then pressed a hand over her mouth. There was no doubt she was the other woman. And the venom in Rachel's voice was terrifying. No wonder Grace feared her mother's rages. Cassie dropped to the straw, her entire body shaking.

"It's the only way," Santiago said. "You'll have everything you ever wanted."

"But he'll just turn around and make more money. And they'll be happy. He always loved that woman. I'd like to kill *her* and see how miserable he is."

"That would be a bad idea." Santiago spoke matter-of-factly, as if he routinely discussed the pros and cons of murder. "You're the ex-wife with a history. The first person they'd look at. You'd end up in prison."

"I said I'd like to kill her," Rachel said, her voice more composed now. "Obviously I'd be caught. But if Alex dies, Grace inherits everything. And I am her mother."

"You can't kill Alex."

"I'm not," Rachel said. "You are."

They were so close, Cassie heard Santiago's patient sigh. "Rachel, you pay me a lot of money but I'm certainly not going to kill him—"

"Walk to the office," she said. "That's where he'll find us having sex. He was still in love with me. Naturally you two fought." Her giggle was high pitched and rather eerie in the cavernous aisle. "I do like the idea of two handsome men dying for me."

"Good God, Rachel. That's not—"

"Don't talk. Just move."

"No, I'm leaving."

"Then I'll shoot you here." Rachel's voice was more level now, crisp with purpose.

Cassie pressed her disbelieving hand tighter over her mouth. This couldn't be happening. Santiago and Rachel were friends, teammates and quite possibly lovers. There was no way she'd shoot him.

Santiago didn't appear to believe Rachel's threat either. He seemed amazingly cool, shrugging as he strode toward the office. Neither of them looked sideways. And that was fortunate because if they glanced at the end stall, they would have noticed a strange horse eating hay.

However, when they left the office, they'd be staring directly at Freckles. They wouldn't miss him then. And they'd look in the stall, wondering about the horse, and they'd discover her hiding place…and realize Grace was also on the property.

Cassie gulped. If only Freckles were smaller. Or lying down.

She unbuckled her belt, crept across the straw and wrapped the narrow leather strap around his neck. Her boss had trained this horse. Maybe she could duplicate the commands. But she didn't have a stick to tap his knees and Freckles was contentedly eating hay, not anticipating going to work.

"Down, boy," she whispered. *Please.* She tugged at the belt around his neck and at the same time tapped his knees with her hand. But he only stared in confusion, a piece of hay protruding from the side of his mouth.

Despair swept her. It wasn't going to work. And she didn't know the last movie he was in, or what training was fresh in his mind. Maybe he needed to be prompted by a whip or a whistle or clapping. It could be anything.

At least he'd stopped chewing. He was studying her now as if he realized she wanted something. And he was a very obliging horse. Even if she didn't copy his cues exactly, it was obvious he wanted to please.

She tugged his head downward again, tapped his left leg and this time clucked. He eyed her for a second then tentatively lowered his head and bowed. Her relief was so sharp, she wanted to hug him. But it wasn't enough. His head was down but his big rump was still visible over the stall door.

She remained crouching, and gave another tug and tap. He stretched out his front legs and ponderously lay down, even flattening his head against the hay, too obedient to even try to eat. *You wonderful horse.* No one would see them now and he looked relaxed, as if prepared to hold his position for hours.

She wouldn't need hours though, she thought, as she settled down beside his prone head. Santiago would talk some sense into Rachel, and the woman would put away the gun and think a little more about Alex's offer. And there'd be no more crazy threats about killing people.

Although Alex really needed to hear Rachel's true feelings about Grace.

Cassie pulled her phone from her back pocket, pressed RECORD and held it close to the stall mesh. Maybe it would pick up the conversation in the office. She'd certainly been wrong about Santiago. She should have know Alex would have a man in place, watching over Grace. No doubt Santiago was relaying everything to Alex, protecting his interests, watching over his daughter. And Alex had mentioned a safeguard—

Pop. The sound was foreign in the serene barn. For a moment, Cassie couldn't process what she'd heard.

Then the phone dropped from her nerveless fingers, her throat so dry it was impossible to breathe. She stared in terror at Freckles, at his soft and trusting eyes. He lifted his head as if questioning whether he should get up.

Oh, God. Fear galvanized her and she pressed his head back in the straw. He gave a resigned sigh that sounded horrifyingly loud. She crouched by the horse, every nerve taut, praying she'd hear Santiago's voice again. But it was silent.

She plucked her fallen phone from the straw and sent a frantic message to Alex. *I think Rachel just shot Santiago!*

Somehow the words made it seem unbearably real, and

she pressed the cell phone against her chest, the sound of her heartbeat thrashing in her ears.

Freckles' nostrils flared, picking up on her distress. He raised his head again but she pushed it back. This was no longer a game, with a verbal whiplashing from Rachel the only penalty. This was terrifyingly real. She was alone in the enemy's barn, hiding thirty feet from a mad woman.

CHAPTER THIRTY-EIGHT

The minutes crawled past. Cassie pulled in another shallow breath, her hand pressed against Freckles' neck, warning him to remain flat in the straw. She didn't know if Rachel had left the office or how much time had passed since the gunshot. But it felt interminable.

She couldn't hear any sounds although thick aisle rubber would muffle footsteps, making it impossible to guess Rachel's location. It felt like the woman was close though, judging from the goose bumps chilling Cassie's neck. No way was she leaving the stall. She and Freckles would be fine if they just remained low.

And then Freckles swished his tail, the rustle of straw startlingly loud. For a second Cassie quit breathing. She stared at the top of the door, expecting to see Rachel's face loom over the stall. But everything remained silent. There was still no noise from the aisle. Or the office.

Her phone vibrated. She jerked her head back down and scanned Alex's newest message: *Santiago is fine. He just sent me a text. Wants to meet in the office. Rachel has agreed to sign.*

Relief swept her, such a warm and welcoming flood that her shoulders slumped against the thick boards. So the popping noise hadn't been a gunshot. It seemed

Santiago had convinced Rachel to accept the offer. Maybe they'd been opening champagne. Perhaps they were kissing now and that would explain why it was so quiet…although it was odd he'd embrace a woman who'd just threatened to shoot him. And Rachel had sounded deadly serious. There'd been no mistaking her rage when she accused Santiago of betrayal.

Cassie typed another message to Alex. *Does Santiago give you private reports about Grace and the stable? If so, I think Rachel found out. She sounded furious.*

Damn, Alex wrote. *I better call him. Stay hidden.*

She edged closer to Freckles' solid presence, stroking his neck while she absorbed this new information. Alex hadn't denied that Santiago worked for him. Which explained why he'd trusted the man with Grace's safety. An elite polo player who doubled as a pseudo protector would be expensive, but she should have guessed Alex would have security in place. Little wonder Rachel was enraged. She'd thought Santiago was her man. Everyone had.

A phone blared from the office. Cassie tilted her head, listening for the deep rumble of Santiago's voice. But the phone rang six times, unanswered. The noise was replaced with tomblike silence.

She rocked forward, staggered by the realization that Santiago had really been shot. Rachel must have sent Alex that message.

Freckles was eyeing her with a look of concern. She flattened her hand back over his neck, drawing comfort from his presence but needing him to remain quiet, now more than ever.

Her phone vibrated. She snatched it up and stared at

Alex's text: *Santiago's not answering. Can you hear his phone?*

Yes, she typed, her fingers so numb with fear they fumbled over the tiny keys. *It's ringing from the office. Call an ambulance. And the police. But stay away from the barn. Rachel wants to kill you.*

Are you safe? Alex wrote.

Yes. Just get Grace. Rachel is unstable. She wants to hurt you, any way she can. Cassie stared in disbelief at the words she'd typed, hating to accept that Santiago had really been shot. No wonder Alex had always hurried home before the man left. With Santiago around, Grace had never been unprotected.

Are you still in the back stall? Alex asked. *Can you get out?*

No. She tapped out a frantic reply. *Rachel is too close. I think she's in the office. She's waiting for you. But it's a trap. Stay away.*

Seconds later Alex's text filled her screen: *I'm coming. When you hear my car, run to the poolhouse and hide with Grace. Wait for the police. They'll be there soon, love always.*

She blinked in horror. What was he planning? It was almost like he was saying goodbye. She expected he'd speed to Grace, but naturally he'd want to help Santiago. The poor man might still be alive. And Rachel could remain holed up in the office for hours, forcing the police and ambulance to remain outside…with Cassie and Freckles caught in any crossfire.

But Alex wasn't thinking clearly. Rachel had a gun while he was unarmed. He couldn't just stroll into the barn and ask to check on Santiago's health.

Don't come here! she texted. *It's too dangerous. Rachel plans to kill you so Grace will inherit everything. And afterwards Grace won't be safe either.*

She trembled, gripping her phone with both hands, willing him to answer. But the screen remained empty.

Clearly he didn't understand the situation. She gave a frustrated sob, knowing she had to risk calling him. Make him understand that Rachel had turned deadly. She pressed his number, then turned her mouth closer to the wall and wet her throat, trying to gather enough saliva for a whisper. Her mouth was so dry, so parched with fear—

Straw rustled and hooves thumped as a big body shifted.

She dropped her phone, realizing too late that she'd removed her hand from Freckles' neck and he'd assumed it was time to get up. He was standing above her now, straw entwined in his mane...and her beige belt dangling oddly from his neck.

Her chest pounded so hard it hurt. She didn't want to get up. Wanted to burrow beneath the straw and wait until the police arrived. But she had to convince Freckles to lie back down. And the belt around his neck was much too noticeable.

She rose on shaky legs. Peered up and down the empty aisle then edged to his side. His eyes turned hopeful, as if anticipating a reward for a trick well done. She gave him a silent pat and tugged downward on the belt. He blew out a sigh, reluctant to lie back down but too sweet-natured to protest. Then his ears pricked as his attention switched to something behind her.

Cassie's hand froze over the belt. She turned, swept with a horrible feeling of dread.

Rachel stood in the doorway of the office. The woman didn't move or speak. She just stared, as if in disbelief. Then her teeth bared in a smile and she raised a steel-gray gun. "It seems my plan needs some adjustment," she said. "But this will work. I can't wait to see Alex's face when he finds out all that he lost today."

Cassie's heart pounded in terror. She should duck, maybe jump sideways so Freckles wouldn't be shot too, but her frozen legs felt disconnected to her brain. She could only clutch at Freckles' mane. And stare into the dark muzzle of the gun.

"Is that the horse you two found together?" Rachel's nostrils flared. "Did you really think he'd be welcome here? That I would tolerate a constant reminder?" She shook her head, her chest rising and falling with her rapid breathing.

"He'll have to go too, of course," she said. "But not today." She gestured with her gun. "Now step out of there. Alex never realized you and Santiago were having an affair. But don't worry. Grace and I will mourn you all…"

Her mouth was still moving but Cassie could no longer understand her words. She couldn't hear anything but a dull roaring.

And then a silver convertible launched through the entrance. It screeched down the aisle, skidding across the rubber. Slid sideways and jerked to a stop in front of the office.

Alex leaned over the side, swinging his polo mallet in an avenging arc. The gun flew from Rachel's hand. Freckles flinched, momentarily startled. But he didn't move his feet, remaining rock solid as if aware Cassie needed his support.

Everything seemed to move in slow motion, but conversely at blazing speed. The car shivered and stalled, Rachel was kneeling and holding her wrist, and Alex held the gun.

And then he was there, running his hands over Cassie's head, her neck, her shoulders. "Are you shot?" he asked, his face blazing with an intensity she'd never seen, his irises so dark his eyes looked black. "Where are you hurt?"

"I'm okay," she managed. "Check Santiago."

He nodded. "Stay here."

It was impossible to move. Tremors wracked her body and she simply clung to Freckles, gasping for air, even as Alex yanked a screeching Rachel into the office and out of sight. Minutes later grim-faced officers swarmed the barn followed by two men running with a white medical stretcher.

And then Alex was beside her again, carefully cocooning her in the zebra-striped cooler he pulled from the straw.

"How's Santiago?" she asked, her tongue thick.

"Shot in the chest," Alex said, his eyes still an odd color. "But they think he'll make it. Thanks to you." And then he was holding her and she still found it hard to breathe, but perhaps that was because of his viselike grip or the stink of burnt rubber or because Freckles kept tickling her neck with his whiskers.

"God, I'm sorry," he said. "Rachel… I didn't expect… I'm so sorry."

"You shouldn't have come," she said. "Shouldn't have risked it."

His arms tightened even more and she could feel the pounding of his heart, his ragged breathing, his utter agony.

"I'm okay," she said quickly, trying to ease his guilt.

"That was so brave. Coming in like that with only a polo mallet. And that was a high risk shot... Not even one you practiced."

But despite her attempt to make light of the situation, her voice quavered. Because she knew what would have happened if he hadn't arrived when he did. If he had chosen to remain at the poolhouse with Grace. If he'd been mere seconds slower.

He didn't say anything, just cupped her face and stared into her eyes. She could feel the shaking of his thick palms. "I was so scared," he whispered. "When Santiago didn't answer. He's a good man, capable. So I knew it was bad. I pushed that car for everything it had... It almost wasn't enough."

And then she realized how he'd arrived so quickly. He hadn't stopped at the poolhouse. "So you didn't stop and check on Grace?" she said. "You came right here?"

"Of course," he said simply. "You needed me more."

And though the air was still acrid with the stink of rubber, somehow her chest felt lighter, the air sweeter. And despite the odd presence of a car twisted in the barn aisle, everything seemed normal again. Optimistic even.

Freckles seemed to realize the show was over and that his services were no longer required. He stepped away from Cassie's side and resumed eating hay. Two officers lingered outside the stall, keen to take her statement but clearly loath to rush a man as important as Alex. And he needed to hurry to the poolhouse and somehow explain all the emergency vehicles to his daughter.

The guilt emanating from his taut body made her ache, and she knew there'd be challenging times ahead. However, her last reservations about making a life with

Alex and Grace disappeared. Because it was obvious his arms were big enough to hold them both.

EPILOGUE

The appreciative crowd roared in delight as Alex stretched over Ginger's shoulder and hooked Santiago's mallet, preventing a tie-breaking goal. The two men were putting on an amazing show, demonstrating a level of polo play not usually seen at the Annual Family Tournament. The winner of this game would have bragging rights for the entire year although it was widely expected that a professional like Santiago would carry his team to a last-minute victory.

Cassie still didn't think it fair that Santiago played for the Jonathon Stiles team—after all, Santiago lived in the Sutherland poolhouse—but Alex had just chuckled and said Family Day was meant to be fun and a chance to encourage others to try the sport.

As if the two men weren't both playing to win.

She gave a wry smile. She'd grown to like and respect Santiago but Alex had told him not to hold back, and the Argentinean was clearly playing for his bonus. He pressed his horse into Ginger's shoulder, bumping the mare off the ball and repaying Alex with a skillful maneuver of his own. The two men were the definition of aggressive, both well mounted, both undeniably talented.

It had taken almost a year for Santiago to recover from the gunshot wound, but he was back in the saddle now and clearly as good as ever. Alex confided it wasn't the first time Santiago had been shot and in the man's line of work he suspected it wouldn't be the last.

She'd never imagined there'd be a demand for investigators like Santiago but she was learning a lot about the lifestyle of the truly rich. With Santiago's impressive polo credentials, he had entry into the highest social circles, where he could discreetly report on philandering husbands or murderous ex-wives.

But while Santiago had consulted for Alex in the past, his credentials weren't earning him any passes today. The two men might be friends, but right now they were in a dogfight, battling grimly for possession. The umpire whistled down the play, ruling that Santiago had unfairly impeded Alex and crossed the line of the ball.

Cassie wheeled Digger, checking the scoreboard as she put him in position for a pass. The garish sponsorship sign had been removed and now the bottom of the board simply stated: PONHOOK POLO CLUB WELCOMES ALL. The club executive had decided it wasn't seemly to have a scoreboard sponsored by a woman imprisoned for attempted murder. Both Alex and Grace had agreed.

The scoreboard showed there wasn't much time left in the game, just under a minute. Hopefully it wouldn't need overtime. She, Alex and Grace were well conditioned but Gramps was the fourth member of their team and despite his doctor's assurances, she couldn't help but worry about his stamina.

And his position on the field.

She smiled over her shoulder at her grandfather. Gramps tended to rove a little too much, not sticking to his defensive position but more focused on using the game as a training opportunity. He was always analyzing their horses' play, devising new drills to keep them sharp and happy. Right now, he seemed to think that spooky Tex needed a closer look at the group of kids cheering on the sidelines, sporting a colorful pony club banner.

Gramps grinned at her as he cantered past. "Those two are sure well matched," he called, jabbing his mallet in the direction of Alex and Santiago who were positioning for a free hit. "But I think Alex has the better horse." He smiled approvingly at Ginger, as usual more interested in the horses than the players.

Cassie nodded agreement. In fact her grandfather had trained all the Sutherland horses competing in this last chukka, and if Ginger didn't win Best Playing Pony it would be a surprise. Gramps conducted all his training at the estate now but refused to move into the mansion, insisting on returning to his farmhouse every evening. Often Grace rode back with him.

"It's really nice at your grandfather's," Grace had said. "And he lets all the cats come inside. One night I had three sleeping on my bed."

Cassie glanced up the field, checking on Grace. While Gramps floated around the pitch, the girl could be trusted to play her position. And she was still as kind as ever, sharing Gramps' love of animals and developing a new confidence. She even helped Cassie teach riding lessons and had also participated in a polo demo for her pony club friends. Of course, it was hard not to be confident when one rode a dependable horse like Freckles.

Like Grace, Freckles' attention was pinned on the play. Grace had been assigned the offensive position and a big number '1' was emblazed on the back of her Sutherland uniform. However, from the start of the game Jocelyn Stiles had shadowed Grace, pushing her around as though it were a huge coup to outplay an eleven-year-old.

Even though Grace hadn't touched the ball much, she was still grinning, happy to be playing in the championship game and thrilled that the proceeds were going to animal rescue. However, Cassie felt a mother's indignation at the way Jocelyn bullied Grace, taking advantage of the girl's inexperience.

Even Freckles flattened his ears, tired of being crowded and intent on protecting his rider's space. It was obvious he'd do his job at putting Grace in the proper position, if only Jocelyn would give them some room. Freckles was so brave, so bold.

The ball was back in play, with Alex and Santiago a blur of movement. Cassie abruptly turned Digger and galloped toward the left, shaking off her opposing rider. If Alex could reach the ball first, he might manage one last pass before time ran out. And because Gramps had moved to the side of the field, he'd drawn another Stiles player with him, opening up even more ground.

She pictured the play in her mind, telegraphing her thoughts to Alex as clearly as they'd done since childhood. And when speedy Ginger outran Santiago's horse, Alex reached down and backhanded the ball without a second glance.

It was a perfect no-look pass that dropped in front of Digger as though positioned by radar. She tapped it off the planked sideboard, pushing it ahead with her mallet. She could hear Santiago wheeling and pounding up the field, intent on stopping her team's last charge. She tapped the ball forward, using Digger's agility to play with the ball, drawing in both Jonathon Stiles and his brother.

Then. "Go, Grace!" she called.

She swung, pulling back her mallet and lobbing the ball high in the air. It dropped twenty feet in front of the goalposts, a sphere of white rolling benignly over the grass.

Freckles was already moving in pursuit with Grace leaning over his neck and urging him on. But Jocelyn's polo pony was much faster. Jocelyn overtook Grace in five strides, guiding her horse into Freckles' shoulder and bullying them off the ball. The crowd groaned. All day, they'd been cheering on the kids, and Grace was the youngest rider of all. They would have loved to see her score the winning goal.

Boos and jeers came from the vocal tailgate section. "Give the kid a chance," someone called. "It's fun day," a deep-voiced man hollered. And the Pony Club children were chanting some sort of ritualistic tune that Grace often hummed.

Freckles seemed to understand that he was in the spotlight. And he was a proven performer. He lowered his head, collected his weight, and *whack!* He body-slammed Jocelyn's horse so hard in the shoulder that the animal flinched, then shrank back, wanting no more competition over a mere plastic ball.

Freckles shifted, smoothly positioning Grace so she could hit the ball with her right hand. He even slowed to a trot as if realizing there were only seconds left on the clock and this was a very critical shot. Grace took aim, swung and the ball bounced between the white posts. The goal judge waved a flag over his head, signifying a goal, and the crowd erupted.

Alex and Santiago galloped up beside Cassie, both of them grinning.

"Nice pass, sweetheart," Alex said, leaning over and tapping Cassie's helmet. "Did you two practice that?"

"Yes, they did," Santiago said. He ruefully pumped their hands. "I spotted them practicing that last week. That's why I had Jocelyn shadowing her. But the kid has come a long way. That was quite a ride-off. Good on you all."

Cassie made a mental note not to practice plays when Santiago was in residence. But she couldn't stop smiling. Because they *had* come a long way. And just seeing the happiness on Alex's face left her light with a shared joy.

The crowd's claps intensified, their whistles and laughter followed by a groundswell of applause. She glanced around in confusion. Even accounting for Grace's enthusiastic friends, the cheering was far more vigorous than normal. The tournament trophy wasn't even in sight. That was scheduled to be presented later, during the community barbecue.

"I believe Ginger just lost Best Playing Pony," Alex said, reaching out and squeezing Cassie's knee. "At least in popular opinion."

She followed his twinkling eyes to where Grace and Freckles remained in front of the goalposts.

Clearly the horse was a natural born showboat who hadn't forgotten his movie cues. And while the young girl who'd never wanted to ride in public laughed and waved at her friends, Freckles was totally hamming it up by dropping bows to the captivated crowd.

ABOUT THE AUTHOR

Bev Pettersen is a three-time nominee in the National Readers Choice Award and a two-time finalist in the Romance Writers of America's Golden Heart® Contest, as well as the recipient of many other international writing awards. She competed for five years on the Alberta Thoroughbred race circuit and is an Equine Canada certified coach. She lives in Nova Scotia with her family—humans and four-legged—and when not writing novels, she's riding. If you want to know when her next book will come out, please visit her at www.BevPettersen.com

www.ingramcontent.com/pod-product-compliance
Lightning Source LLC
Chambersburg PA
CBHW060515080526
44586CB00012B/490